CONTENTS

INTRODUCTION

The inclusion of Outdoor and Adventurous Activities (OAA) in three out of four key stages (KS) of the National Curriculum (NC) for PE is an indication of the value placed by leading educationalists, the Office for Standards in Education (OFSTED) and the Department for Education (DFE) on the undisputed benefits of stimulating experiences gained outside of the classroom in challenging learning situations. Such activities will call on the individual to overcome physical and emotional difficulties, work with and trust others, and develop a respect for the natural world.

Note Although now no longer a requirement at KS1 PE, the orientation activities are seen as an effective means of fulfilling elements of the Programmes of Study (PoS) for KS1 Geography. A section of this book has been devoted to these activities. Similarly, teachers in middle schools will be required to deliver PoS related to KS3. Relevant activities have also been included. The PoS for KS3 OAA is less prescriptive than at KS2, providing scope for the teacher to cover aspects of the KS2 activities that may not have been pursued at KS2 through limitations in time or resources.

In KS2, the PoS for OAA is a compulsory module and thus must be included in the overall programme for PE up to the age of 11. I hope that hard-pressed teachers of KS2 attempting to cope with NC PoS for a whole range of curricular disciplines will welcome this book as an aid in satisfying this aspect without undue complication. My philosophy has been to keep it simple, to make the information 'teacher-friendly'. I am sure teachers will find this work both great fun

and rewarding to see the positive way in which children tackle the activities and respond to the adventure and challenge.

Where several activities are detailed for a particular PoS, the teacher can chose to do one or more to suit his or her own circumstances. The activities outlined have been designed to fulfil the PoS without the need to undertake specialised In-Service Training (INSET) to acquire nationally recognised qualifications in hazardous OAA.

It is important to understand that OAA (encompassing recognised outdoor pursuits, adventure sports and development games) are a vital aspect of outdoor education in general. Outdoor education in its purest definition is any educational activity that takes place outside the formal classroom, a strategy for learning in all NC subjects, endorsed by the School Curriculum and Assessment Authority (SCAA), formerly the National Curriculum Council.

The National Association for Outdoor Education (NAOE) – address on page 95 – is an organisation from which teachers of outdoor education can seek information and guidance. The NAOE defines outdoor education as: 'A means of approaching educational objectives through guided, direct experience in the environment, using its resources as learning materials' (1970). Following the announcement of the foundation subjects and as a result of considerable pressure from many outdoor education representatives, the Secretary of State for Education issued instructions to the SCAA working party for PE to advise on PoS related to OAA. In 1991 the DFE stated that:

'In OAA pupils apply physical and judg-mental skills in different contexts, develop-ing knowledge and experience of moving in different, challenging and changing environments.'

The proven educational benefits for pupils experiencing a course of this nature have been acknowledged for many years:

• personal, moral and social development
• increased understanding of and respect for the environment
• improved health and satisfying use of lei-sure time from cultivating interests in adventure sports such as climbing, absei-ling, mountaineering, paragliding, hang gliding, caving, canoeing, sailing, windsur-fing, orienteering, mountain biking, walk-ing, gliding, skiing, rafting, scuba diving, rowing, horse riding and angling (as recog-nised by the DFE).

The following outcomes in pupil de-velopment are all possible through involve-ment with OAA. (This list is useful at parents' evenings when attempting to jus-tify the activities to sceptical parents!)

Development of:
• character
• increased confidence
• determination and perseverance
• self-discipline
• self-awareness and integrity
• tolerance of others
• social awareness and interest in the wel-fare of others
• unselfish, compassionate attitudes
• leadership
• initiative and self-motivation
• respect for the environment

• awareness of conservation and pollution issues
• community spirit
• humility and respect for others
• self-respect and dignity.

The ingredients of any outdoor adventure experience comprise varying levels of psychological, physiological and technical expertise. These commodities may provide a useful means of assessment:

• the affective domain – feelings, emotions aroused through the activity (satisfaction, awe, joy, response to challenge); the PSME (personal, social, moral education) content
• psychomotor dexterity – hand-eye-brain co-ordination developed through the physi-cal skill-based nature of some of the activities
• cognitive knowledge – acquired to solve problems, prepare and plan for journeys and activities.

Adventure-based activities rely on the presence of a physical or psychological challenge for pupils to overcome. The pres-ence of a challenge implies the presence of risk, which in turn implies the presence of danger to some degree or other. Danger-ous activities are hard to justify education-ally unless one can show that all possible steps to eliminate the danger have been taken, and DFE codes of practice are being followed.

In determining what constitutes an 'acceptable risk' one must analyse danger more thoroughly. Subjective danger is that which can be controlled by the supervisor through correct choice of venue to suit the abilities of the participants, the assessment of weather and its effect on the activity, the correct application of safety techniques, good leadership, and strict adherence to recommendations in the DFE publication 'Safety in Outdoor Education'. Objective danger is that which lies to some extent outside the control of the supervisor, e.g. a lightning strike, an avalanche, a rockfall, etc. However, even these events can be avoided by understanding the physical conditions associated with these phenomena. Clearly at KS1 and KS2 level the objective danger is minimal, whereas a Himalayan expedition represents obvious and ever present dangers.

Furthermore, danger can be perceived as that which is deemed to be real and life-threatening, e.g. 'If you walk too close to the edge of that cliff you will fall', and that which is apparent to the individual but is not necessarily life-threatening, e.g. a pupil on the end of a climbing rope. The pupil may feel that if he slips he will fall to the ground, when in reality he should be held by the belayer(s) at the other end.

In staging adventure learning situations we should note that there are four recognised levels of adventure threshold which may be experienced by an individual. The point at which an individual will reach a particular threshold is peculiar to his or her experience, familiarity with the activity, training and understanding, personality, etc.

• **Level 1 Recreation** – little stimulation, boredom, arising out of an activity that has minimal challenge or enjoyment. For example, a group of 11 year olds being led on a walk around the school premises with no pupil-based tasks.

• **Level 2 Adventure** – minimal arousal resulting from repetition or a challenge set well below the pupils' abilities. For example, a bouldering (low-level) climbing exercise on a frame or wall that does not call on the pupil to think about the correct moves to reach a predetermined point on the frame.

• **Level 3 Frontier adventure** – maximum arousal, full concentration and employment of mental and physical attributes to overcome a new, stimulating challenge. For example, a rope trail through a forest in darkness.

• **Level 4 Misadventure** – genuine fear, anxiety, inability to cope with a very real danger that has arisen through an inappropriate challenge. For example, leading a group up or down a cliff face where the possibility of safeguarding a fall is impracticable.

Clearly then, pitching the activity at the appropriate level for a particular group can be an extremely difficult task. As the teacher acquires more experience and understanding of the group, then this task becomes more manageable.

In practice, with mixed ability groups it is not at all easy to cater for all thresholds. The more confident pupils can be given extra responsibility or asked to help others. **The golden rule is that the activity must be pitched at the level of the weakest group member**. I have attempted to help the supervising teacher in this respect through the format of the suggested activities in this book. For those teachers working with children with special needs, I have included a section with suggestions on how to cope with differing disabilities. However, I feel that specialist Special Educational Needs (SEN) teachers are better equipped to design their own strategies having seen what activities are possible to fulfil the PoS.

In writing this book I have tried to illustrate how the PoS for KS2 (and KS3) may be fulfilled effectively by non-specialist teachers without recourse to extensive (and expensive!) INSET to satisfy DFE/LEA Health and Safety codes of practice in recognised adventure sports such as climbing, canoeing, etc. However, if your school is in a position to offer such activities, either from within (if suitable resources and qualified staff are available) or through outside agencies, then the programme and its outcomes will be enhanced. In dealing with these hazardous adventure activities I have indicated what I would constitute a suitable strategy for teachers who fulfil their LEA's supervisory requirements.

Most LEAs will provide an 'in county' system of training and accreditation at 'taster' level. Details can be obtained from your PE Adviser or General Education Inspector.

There is a wide range of adventure activities currently available through outside agencies and private country centres. The canoeing tragedy at Lyme Bay has served to highlight the fact that private centres do not necessarily have to comply with DFE recommendations. Following this tragedy, the DFE has stated that the responsibility for assessing the safety aspects of an outside agency lies solely with the school. I have therefore included a section on outside agencies – a checklist of good practices to look for when deciding to use these services.

It goes without saying that even with the limited exposure to danger that KS2 (and KS3) activities will present, the challenging nature of the activities must be acknowledged. It is most important for supervising staff to be alert to any possible hazards and plan accordingly. Strict regimes of discipline and organisation are essential. Further advice for each activity along with a general appraisal of what the teacher should consider with regard to safety and supervision is given throughout the book.

KS2 teachers may wish to explore and exploit the potential for learning with OAA from cross-curricular themes, e.g. a planned day of canoeing on a lake may relate to classroom studies on the 'water cycle'. I have indicated any possibilities for these links to take place in the activities described.

Finally, the strong links between OAA and residential experience deserve recognition and attention. Although there is no statutory requirement for a residential experience at KS2 (or KS3), a school may wish to pursue this further opportunity to promote PSME. Residential experience requires children to adapt and respond to unfamiliar routines, environments and social groupings. Furthermore, a sense of purpose and focus of specific stimuli can be achieved in the rarefied atmosphere of a residential setting. When linked to residential experience, OAA can develop social learning skills through the challenging, team building, socially aware and interdependent nature of the situation, highlighting how an overnight standing camp, bivouac or stay in a youth hostel may be planned.

RECORD OF ACHIEVEMENT

Physical Education – Key Stage 2
Outdoor and Adventurous Activities

Pupil ....

Key Stage Descriptions

A Experience Outdoor and Adventurous Activities in different environments (school grounds, parks, woodlands, seashore, open country) that involve planning, navigating, working in small groups, recording and evaluating.

B Experience challenges of a problem-solving nature, using suitable equipment, that include planning, recording and evaluating while working in groups.

C Be taught the skills necessary for the activities.

KS Descr.	Activity	Location	Date	Attainment (A – E)				Comments
				Y3	Y4	Y5	Y6	

SELF-ASSESSMENT SHEET

1 What has been the biggest contribution you have made during these activities?

2 What have you found the most difficult to cope with?

3 What do you think you have gained from the course?

4 What have you learnt about your own capabilities?

5 How well do you feel you performed?

6 Is there anything you could have improved on?

7 Have you changed your views on other people in the group? If so, how and why?

8 Who in the group impressed you and why?

9 What have you learnt about working in a group?

10 What has been your group's greatest strengths and weaknesses?

11 Which activity have you enjoyed the most and why?

12 Which activity, if any, have you disliked and why?

THE PoS AND ATTAINMENT TARGET

KS1

(A) Simple orientation activities suitable for Geography KS1.

(1) Scavenger hunts.
(2) Observation trails.
(3) Treasure hunts.
(4) Simple mapping exercises.
(5) Basic orienteering.

KS2

(A) Pupils should be taught outdoor and adventurous activities in different environments (school grounds and premises, parks, woodland or seashore).

(1) Adventure games.
• Smugglers.
• Hide and seek.
• Stalking.
• Rope trails.
• Blindfold trust games.
• Blindfold confidence games.
(2) Nature trails and scavenger hunts.
(3) Confidence courses and activity trails.
(4) Orienteering.
(5) Walks and rambles.
(6) Camping and bivouacking.
(7) Visits to the seaside (coastal activities).

(B) Pupils should be taught challenges of a problem-solving nature, using suitable equipment, which include planning, recording and evaluating whilst working in small groups.

• Centipede.
• Acid stream.

• Square dance.
• Retrieving the bucket.
• Dots and lines.
• Reef knot around the tree.
• Filling the leaking container.
• Raft building and rafting on placid water.

(C) Pupils should be taught the skills necessary for the activities undertaken.

(1) Walks and rambles.
• Conservation considerations.
• Map reading skills.
• General safety appropriate to the activity.
• Walking skills.
• Getting fit for the journey.
• Winter activities.
• Information relating to the area to be visited.
(2) Orienteering.
(3) Camping and bivouacking.
(4) Visits to the seaside (coastal activities).

KS3

At KS3 OAA is an optional area of activity which may be pursued as a half-unit (A) or full unit (A + B).

Unit A

Pupils should be taught:
(a) one or more OAA, either on or off the school site
(b) the techniques and skills specific to the activities undertaken.
Suggested activities from KS2 PoS: (C1) walks and rambles; (C2) orienteering; (C3) camping and bivouacking.

Unit B

Pupils should be taught:
(c) at least one other OAA to include, where possible, offsite work in unfamiliar environments.
Suggested activities from KS2 PoS: as per Unit A.

Pupils should be taught:
(d) a variety of roles in each activity, including leading, being led and sharing.

Suggested activities from KS2 PoS: (A1) adventure games; (A3) confidence courses and activity trails; (A4) orienteering; (B) problem-solving activities.

Attainment target

The attainment target (AT) for PE is the extent to which pupils fulfil the end of KS descriptions in the PoS.

The treatment of the thorny subject of assessment and recording attainment doesn't have to be over-elaborate and time-consuming to be effective and representative of the PoS and AT. The strategies of planning-performing-evaluating lend themselves well to the activities prescribed in this book.

To recap, let us not forget that attainment in PE is the extent to which pupils fulfil the end of KS descriptions in the PoS. In addition to this, let us not forget that when we look for criteria to assess in OAA, we can analyse the activity in terms of its cognitive knowledge, psychomotor dexterity and affective emotional response.

Cognitive knowledge can be assessed through the responses to practical assignments offered to the pupils, as well as through the photocopiable pupil resource sheets supplied. Psychomotor dexterity is closely linked to performing. A number of the activities in KS2 (and KS3) will require these skills if the pupil is to succeed in the tasks. Suitable activities include climbing, activity circuits, confidence courses and some of the adventure games. In describing and recognising his response and performance in the activities, the pupil will be satisfying any need for assessment in the affective domain.

Above all, the assessment scheme should be simple to implement and of use to upper school teachers who will be pursuing OAA at KS3 and KS4.

A sample record of achievement sheet appears on page 8, an example of a self-assessment sheet on page 9. The skills can be taken from the aims of each activity, e.g. camping and bivouacking – camping skills; ability to work with others.

KS1 activities (orientation in Geography)

KS: 1.
PoS: Geography.
Activity: scavenger hunts (A1).
Aim: to develop observation skills and search strategies.
Time required: 30–50 minutes.

Location: school playground; school fields.
Equipment: coloured marker discs or similar; possibly cards with names of stations written on them.
Target group: 5–6 year olds. Class of 30 working in groups of 4 or 5.

Teacher's guidance notes

Scavenger hunts will appeal to younger children's inquisitive nature and desire to explore. They can be linked to search and rescue techniques used by rescue organisations. The pupils are asked to work together as a group to find a set number of items within a defined area. You may wish to do some follow-up work on the rescue services. The children could be told what services are available – the telephone directory employs good graphics to depict the various agencies.

The focus for the hunt can be as simple as coloured markers (different colours to be collected). Markers can be situated in as many different stations as their colours, i.e. four colours, four stations.

The first group back with a complete set of markers wins, although you may feel that the competitive element is undesirable. Don't put markers in places of danger, places where children could fall or run into awkward objects.

It may be wise for the first hunt to be relatively straightforward, asking the pupils to collect one marker and informing them where it is hidden. Tell the children that they must move quietly through the school.

Assessment: assess results of hunt.
Cross-curricular links: Citizenship; Health and Fitness.
Pupil resources: none.

KS: 1.
PoS: Geography.
Activity: observation trails (A2).
Aim: to develop observation skills.
Time required: 30–50 minutes.

Location: school grounds.
Equipment: waymarker cards with arrows.
Target group: 6–7 year olds. Class of 30 working in groups of 4.

Teacher's guidance notes

Observation trails follow waymarked routes in a similar way to those found on nature trails in forested areas or other areas of public countryside recreation. If a visit to such an area is possible, then the activity will be stimulating and rewarding for the pupils. However, I suggest that each group is supervised closely by an adult.

The same aims can be achieved within the school grounds by providing home-made waymarkers for the children to follow. Bright backgrounds and the size and direction of the arrows should be given a good deal of thought. The pupils could be involved in repairing the arrows themselves. Staff could fix them to posts with pins, Sellotape, etc.

Set the course up and ask pupils to look for certain items, such as: the number of trees on the trail; the number of red doors you pass; the number of houses you can see. Pupils can record their results on a sheet of paper and hand it in at the end for checking.

As with all activities involving journeys around the school, make sure that children understand that they should not enter other classes or disturb fellow pupils.

The course should be designed so that the pupils can spot the next arrow before leaving the previous, to avoid getting lost and straying into potentially dangerous areas.

Assessment: examine results.
Cross-curricular links: Citizenship; Health and Fitness; Environment.
Pupil resources: none.

KS: 1.
PoS: Geography.
Activity: treasure hunts (A3).
Aim: to develop expertise in following graphical symbols; to provide pupils with an activity which will encourage a sense of discovery and exploration.

Time required: 30–50 minutes.
Location: school grounds.
Equipment: treasures; graphical instructions; plotting compasses, bar magnets.
Target group: 6–7 year olds. Class of 30 working in groups of 4.

Teacher's guidance notes

Treasure hunts are a good way of fulfilling aspects of the Geography PoS which calls on children to 'develop geographical skills based on direct experience, practical activities and exploration of the local area.' Treasure hunts are a stimulating activity for young people, especially if the treasure is worth hunting for! Possible treasures could include sweets, chocolate bars, fruit, etc. Try to arrange for different treasure locations so that each group has a different journey and thus different route-finding problems.

Start with treasure hunts that have simple instructions such as left, right, forwards, backwards. Pupils should be interested as to what is meant by these commands, and be able to identify the commands on the instruction sheet:

Practise these movements until everyone is moving correctly. You could attempt to stage a marching course.

Issue pupils with treasure hunt details and discuss what is meant by a 'pace', i.e. L-R-L = 3 paces (keep it simple).

Pupils are to return to base with treasure as proof of discovery. Advanced learning could relate to the eight points of a compass. A large visual aid could be helpful here to show the eight points. Show the pupils how to turn the direction symbol until it lines up with the North-pointing end of a plotting compass needle. Discuss

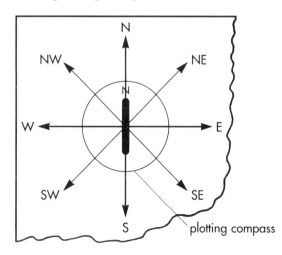

plotting compass

15

the fact that the compass needle always points North because of an invisible attracting force known as magnetism. If possible, put two bar magnets together to show the force of attraction.

Show them how to keep turning the sheet until North lines up. Now the instructions can be given in terms of the eight points of the compass and paces.

Assessment: observation of treasures.
Cross-curricular links: Citizenship; Health and Fitness; Environment; Science.
Pupil resources: instructions.

KS: 1.
PoS: Geography.
Activity: simple mapping exercises (A4).
Aim: to develop observation skills and convert information gained in the field.
Time required: 30–50 minute map-making sessions, plus time for gathering information in the field.

Location: classroom, gymnasium and local sites.
Equipment: pens, pencils, colours, tracing paper, clipboards.
Target group: 5–7 year olds. Class of 30 working individually.

Teacher's guidance notes

Younger pupils can begin with a familiar environment such as the classroom.

(1) The class could gather around a display of shaped blocks, a model of a building or something similar, and try to draw the layout as they see it from their viewpoint. Although all the 'maps' will be different, they are all correct. Now place another object in the display and ask the pupils to mark its position on their maps with an 'X'. Finish with a game of 'follow the leader' in which the teacher moves the figure's path of travel on the children's maps.

(2) Prepare a set of maps showing the centre of the classroom and a piece of furniture or object marked at some other location. Pupils are to locate the object and find the coded letter, return to the teacher and attempt another map. This activity could be repeated in the gymnasium.

(3) The teacher can then go on to ask pupils to imagine that they are looking down on the room. Ask the pupils to visualise how the room would look from above. This is the principle behind a map. Pupils can trace the symbols for the room components and transfer them on to their plan. As with the previous activities, there need not be any reference to scale. The outline plan of any classroom may need to be altered to accommodate any irregularities in the shape of the room that do not correspond to the rectangular shape given on the photocopiable sheet.

(4) Further activities can include walks to local sites, asking the pupils to record the shape of their journey on a blank sheet. Then ask them to make a larger, neater copy back at school. A useful road safety lesson can also be undertaken if the route chosen takes the pupils to places where the road signs on the other blank sheet are encountered. A clipboard is essential for these activities. So is dry weather if you are to have a sporting chance of disseminating the information on return to school.

Assessment: examine the finished plans and maps.
Cross-curricular links: Environment.
Pupil resources: *see* worksheets.

Name _____

Make a plan of your classroom in the box below. Trace the symbols on to your plan in their correct position.

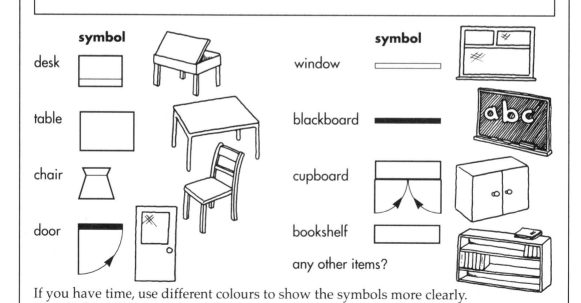

	symbol			symbol	
desk			window		
table			blackboard		
chair			cupboard		
door			bookshelf		
			any other items?		

If you have time, use different colours to show the symbols more clearly.
We call this a 'key' or 'legend'.

Name _____

We are going to walk from school to _____

Draw the route on this sheet. Then copy it out more accurately on a larger sheet of paper back at school.

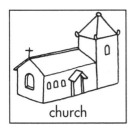

church

police station

fire station

school

supermarket

park

my house

A WALK FROM SCHOOL

Name --

Look for these traffic signs on you journey to ------------------------------------

Mark your route plan with the number of the traffic sign.
Back at school, trace the symbols on to the larger map.

1

What does it mean?

2

What does it mean?

3

What does it mean?

4

What does it mean?

5

What does it mean?

6

What does it mean?

KS: 1.
PoS: Geography.
Activity: orienteering (A5).
Aim: to introduce the sport of orienteering; to develop orientation skills using simple, pictorial maps and large scale plans.

Time required: 30–35 minutes.
Location: school grounds.
Equipment: 3D maps, painted boards.
Target group: 6–7 year olds. Class of 30 working in groups of 4.

Teacher's guidance notes

As with the other activities described in section A, the orientation activities in A5 are most suitable for fulfilling elements of the Geography PoS calling for pupils to 'develop geographical skills based on direct experience, practical activities and exploration of the local area.' In this section we are attempting to begin the process of relating a map to the surroundings – a basic navigational skill which forms the cornerstone of the most demanding navigational situations, e.g. Duke of Edinburgh Award Gold Expeditions.

The maps should be simplistic in design, of large scale and preferably three-dimensional. A simple plan of the school can be converted quite easily into a 3D map with a little imagination and use of simple projection.

A 3D map forms a useful halfway house, a transitional step for the pupils to grasp the relevant concepts before moving on to the use of aerial plans and Ordnance Survey maps in KS2.

Once competence has been achieved with a 3D map, it should be possible to move

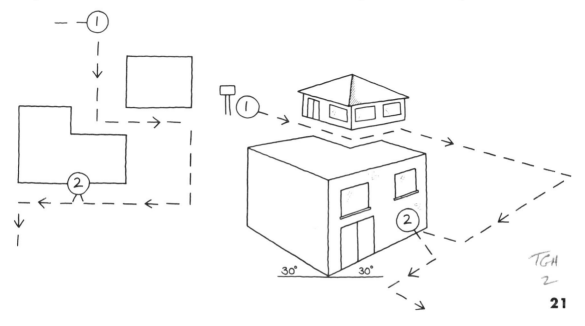

on to simple aerial plans. The maps should show clearly the features that the pupils can easily identify such as the school entrance, gymnasium, classrooms, etc. Do not produce a map with superfluous detail that will clutter and confuse. The pupils should be able to see clearly the paths that they must take to find the orienteering markers (these can take the form of painted boards with an animal picture or something similar for them to identify) and complete the course.

Orienteering is a leisure activity in which participants have a map showing control points. They go to the control points, find the marker board and record the infor-mation on it. Sometimes they race against each other to see who can find them the fastest.

The pupils must be shown how to set the map, i.e. turn the map so that it lines up with the features they can see in front of them.

Do not mention scale at this stage of learning other than to say that everything on the map is a miniature version of its actual size.

You could also ask pupils to measure the length of the course by using pacing as in A3.

Finally, remind pupils of out of bounds, quiet rules as in activities A1, A2 and A3.

Assessment: examine the results.
Cross-curricular links: Citizenship; Health and Fitness; Environment.
Pupil resources: none (teacher to produce own map and result sheet).

KS: 2.
PoS: A.
Activity: adventure games (A1) – smugglers; stalking; hide and seek.
Aim: to develop observational and listening skills; to create opportunities for initiative; to have fun and adventure and thereby develop oneself; to reinforce attributes in teamwork and group co-operation.

Time required: most activities described can be pursued within a 30–35 minute period.
Location: woodland.
Equipment: activity (a) smugglers – containers filled with loot, rope to mark the 'den', whistle, detention compound; activity (b) stalking – none; activity (c) hide and seek – none.
Target group: 8–9 year olds.

Teacher's guidance notes

These games will encourage the pupils to move quietly and work together using sign language to outwit their opponents. Dark clothing and possibly army black-up for the face can add to the sense of adventure and fun.

(a) Smugglers: two teams of 4 or 5 set up their dens approximately 50 metres away in an area of dense woodland. The den should be marked with a rope laid out into a square approximately 10 by 10 metres. This size will give the opponents a sporting chance of penetrating the compound without being caught. Both teams not only have the problem of defending their own den, but they must attempt to infiltrate and capture the other team's treasure, e.g. bars of chocolate. If detected, the pupil caught must be escorted back to a detention point by one of the 'observers'. Decide on a time limit for the game (a whistle is useful for this purpose), after which the result is decided by the number of successful entries into the opponents' den. Each time a group member

is successful, he/she can be exchanged for treasure at the conclusion of the game.

(b) Stalking: teach the children various ways of stalking and creeping up on targets without being detected. Display techniques such as pulling themselves along on their stomachs, hands and knees making shuffling movements, etc. Split the group into pairs, each member of the pair should go to opposite ends of the woodland. The aim is to sneak up on the partner and touch them on the shoulder before they are spotted. Note that children's clothing will become very dirty and possibly torn. It is a good idea to warn pupils of the possibility of twigs penetrating the eye, thorns in fingers, nettle stings, etc. A set of protective glasses, leather gardening gloves and old clothing are recommended. The activity could be followed by a group session in which the group attempts to stalk deer or other elusive forest fauna.

(c) Hide and seek: no introduction is needed to this established adventure game other than to comment that ground rules should be laid down regarding the limits of where the pupils may hide, places of danger to avoid (such as up trees and down holes), etc. Decide on a hiding and searching time limit, whereupon the victim has won if not found. Change roles.

Assessment: direct observation.
Cross-curricular links: Citizenship; Environment.
Pupil resources: none.

KS: 2/3.
PoS: KS2: B; KS3: Unit B(d).
Activity: adventure games – A1 rope trails.
Aim: to develop confidence and trust in others; to appreciate the sense of sight and gain a better understanding of those who are blind.

Time required: 30–50 minutes, depending on the length of the trail and the number in the group.
Location: school playground or field.
Equipment: a length of rope and possibly some climber's slings (simple rope slings will suffice) and karabenas (form of snap link); blindfolds.
Target group: 10–12 year olds.

Teacher's guidance notes

Set up the rope so that the pupils must negotiate a number of obstacles. All obstacles should be positioned a safe height from the ground, about less than a metre. Avoid big drops and sharp, pointed obstacles. Take into account any slippery surfaces as well when designing the course.

If you wish, the rope may be tied off at various points with a figure-of-eight knot, clipped into a climber's karabena and doubled sling which may be threaded through around a post or bar, or simply looped over the top of a post. This will enable the course to be more tortuous and disorientating.

Obstacles could range from natural features such as fallen trees, logs, fences, and small ditches, to steps to hurdle, benches, vaulting box, horse, high jump mat and bar. Try to design a course in which the pupils can go under, through and round obstacles as well as over them.

When the course is ready (the pupils can help set it up), number the pupils 1 or 2. All number 1s are blindfolded (use anything that is available such as scarves, lengths of material, etc.). Pair off a number 1 with a number 2. The number 2s offer only verbal assistance in guiding their partner around the course and over the obstacles. Verbal assistance can relate to the nature of the obstacle and how best to negotiate it. On completion of the course, the pupils can swap roles. Design a new course if time permits.

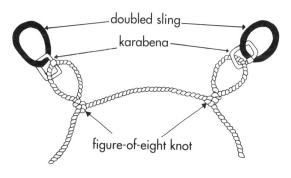

doubled sling

karabena

figure-of-eight knot

Assessment: direct observation.
Cross-curricular links: Health and Fitness; Citizenship.
Pupil resources: none.

KS: 2/3.
Pos: KS2: A; KS3: Unit B(d).
Activity: adventure games – A1 blindfold trust games.
Aim: as in activity A1, also to accommodate each other's performance.

Time required: 30–50 minutes.
Location: playground or school field.
Equipment: various obstacles as in A1 blindfolds.
Target group: 8–12 year olds.

Teacher's guidance notes

(a) Guiding one another round an obstacle course. This is basically the same activity as detailed in A1, but with no rope to guide the pupils. It will encourage the assistants to provide more accurate, detailed verbal instructions to guide successfully. New command of left, right, forwards, backwards can be introduced.

(b) A variation of the above activity is to have a group of pupils moving together, either holding hands or attached to a rope at, say, 1 metre intervals via a large figure-of-eight loop which they can step into to form a waist tie. Prepared ropes with the loops already tied can save a great deal of time. The pupil at the front of the group is the leader, whose task is to coach and lead the rest of the group over the course. The remainder of the group are blindfolded.

Yet another variation is to remove the blindfolds and get the group to move as a team, as smoothly as possible.

Assessment: direct observation.
Cross-curricular links: Health and Fitness; Citizenship.
Pupil resources: none.

KS: 2/3.
PoS: KS2: A; KS3: Unit B(d).
Activity: adventure games A1 blindfold confidence courses.
Aim: to overcome shyness and develop communication skills between pupils.

Time required: 30–50 minutes.
Location: school playground.
Equipment: blindfolds.
Target group: 8–12 year olds. Class of 30 working in groups of 4, then 10.

Teacher's guidance notes

These activities can be a lot of fun for pupils. As with other blindfold activities, the children can come to appreciate the gift of sight and become more aware of the difficulties experienced by those who are blind.

(1) Line pupils up and number them 1–2–3–4, 1–2–3–4, etc. Issue blindfolds and ask the group to disperse in the playground. Place blindfolds over eyes, and inform the number 1s that they are sheep. They may only make the sound of a sheep. Demonstrate noise. Inform the number 2s that they are cows, number 3s that they are pigs, and number 4s that they are donkeys. Now each group member must find one another using the animal sound only.

(2) Number pupils 1–2–3, etc. up to a maximum of 10. Issue blindfolds. Ask the pupils to disperse to form a circle and hold hands (one pupil can remain outside the circle with a blindfold on and guide the others). Now all must put on blindfolds and convert their circle into a straight line where all pupils are in numerical order, i.e. 1 first, 10 last.

Assessment: direct observation.
Cross-curricular links: Citizenship; Health and Fitness.
Pupil resources: none.

KS: 2.
PoS: A.
Activity: nature trails and scavenger hunts A2.
Aim: to provide a stimulating way in which to learn about a specific environment; to develop observational and searching strategies.
Time required: ideally a whole day offsite visit, where the activity takes anything from an hour to half a day.
Location: coastal, country or town parks, forestry commission sites.
Equipment: trail/hunt information material providing details of subjects under scrutiny; pens, pencils, clipboards; weatherproofing clear plastic bags or covering.
Target group: 10–11 year olds.

Teacher's guidance notes

A nature trail quiz or scavenger hunt can be an effective means of increasing children's awareness of a particular environment. The exploration and discovery inherent in the activity will capture the imagination of the children and stimulate their natural instinct for adventure.

The quiz/hunt should have a clearly defined focus, ideally linked to preliminary classroom studies which may have been undertaken prior to the activity. Three examples are offered: (1) a trail quiz based on a country park which has developed a woodland habitat from earlier quarrying activity; (2) a marine scavenger hunt that could be part of a visit to the seaside (combined with C4 Visits to the seaside – see page 69); (3) based on a town 'pocket' park with ironstone quarrying connections and a history of habitation by earlier civilisations, it involves simple map reading, observation and recording.

A simple map, such as those shown in the worksheet, may be useful to indicate the location of answer material. A quiz that includes a scavenger element – hunting for specimens – will add extra spice and fun to the proceedings. Take care, however, not to abuse environments by pillaging resources such as rock specimens, flowers, etc., unless permission has been granted and they can be taken without harming the environment. This can form a nice conservation issue to take up with the pupils.

As with orienteering, close supervision of the pupils may not always be possible. Therefore safeguards should be undertaken to ensure that the environment is safe. Pupils should work in groups of 3 or 4, with a watch to enable them to return to base promptly, and knowledge of what to do in an emergency (see Planning a visit on pages 81–5). Alternatively, it may be wise to restrict the activity to a small area in which close supervision is possible.

Assessment: direct observation of teamwork skills; analysis of recordings.
Cross-curricular links: Geography; History; Health and Fitness; Science; Technology.
Pupil resources: see worksheet.

Hunsbury Hill Country Park

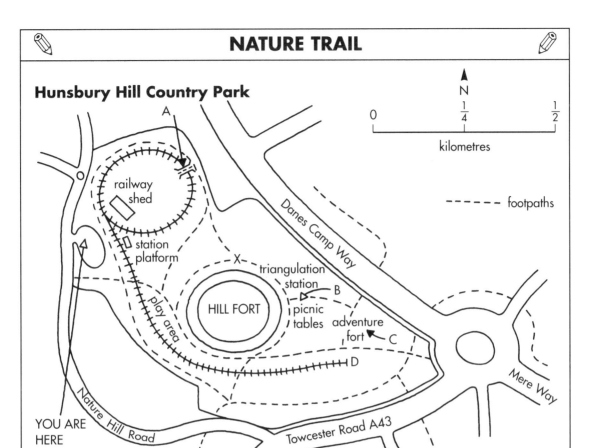

- All groups to visit location X – answer questions.
- Do not cross any main roads.
- Use the footpaths only.

Checkpoints:

A Bridge – How many vertical bars does the bridge have?

B Viewpoint stone – How many picnic tables are there here?

C Adventure fort – List the types of playground equipment.

D Railway terminus – Work out the length of the railway platform using paces.

Questions to be answered at location X:

1 How big is the hill fort?

2 How old is the hill fort?

3 Who built the hill fort?

4 What material has been quarried in this area?

5 What did the early inhabitants of the hill fort store in pits?

6 In the nineteenth century, the railway you have seen was built. What do you think it was used for?

KS: 2/3.
PoS: KS2: A3; KS3: Unit B(d).
Activity: confidence courses and activity trails.
Aim: to develop confidence in one's own abilities and overcome challenging physical problems.
Time required: 60 minutes to half a day.

Location: school grounds, country parks, town parks, forestry recreation areas.
Equipment: ropes, logs, planks, posts, climbing nets, gymnasium equipment, pipes, tunnels, totem climbing poles, stepping stones or blocks.
Target group: 8–12 year olds (according to course difficulty).

Teacher's guidance notes

A confidence or assault course is a trail which requires the student to undertake a number of physical tasks. These may involve an element of risk, suitably safeguarded by safety lines or on-the-spot supervision (*spotting*). Courses of this nature are often to be found at activity centres and army barracks. A growing number are being established at country/forestry recreation sites. Adventure playgrounds in municipal parks are another resource which could be utilised, but a more inventive approach may be necessary here since the park may be familiar to the children. Setting the children tasks on climbing frames, devising activity circuits or utilising trees and bushes (without trespass or damage) may be effective.

On-site confidence courses can be set up in the gym or on the school fields using normal gymnasium equipment. Transporting a log or bench over the course is another option available (assessment in teamwork skills can also take place here).

If a basic strategy of balancing and climbing over, under and through obstacles is maintained, then with a little imagination some challenging courses can be set up. However, it is important to stress the dangers to the children before commencing any activity. Establish a list of dos and don'ts and provide effective supervision – either by leading the group around the circuit and assisting them with potentially dangerous obstacles, or by having helpers posted at various locations. The list of dos and don'ts might be as follows. (**1**) Don't climb so high that you feel you can't climb down or jump off safely (establish a maximum height off the ground with the pupils, and practise jumping-off skills – keep knees bent, aim to land on two feet, jump on to a level surface, jump clear of protruding obstacles). (**2**) Keep clear of moving equipment. (**3**) Stop the equipment moving before attempting to get on or off. (**4**) Hold on to equipment with both hands. (**5**) Don't ignore safety rules or signs.

Assessment: by direct observation.
Cross-curricular links: Environment; Health and Fitness.
Pupil resources: none.

GYMNASIUM CONFIDENCE COURSE

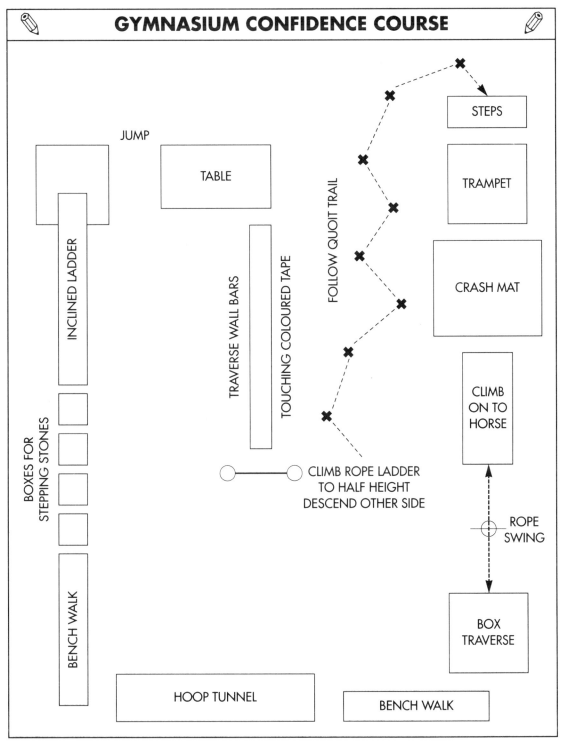

JUMP

TABLE

INCLINED LADDER

TRAVERSE WALL BARS

TOUCHING COLOURED TAPE

FOLLOW QUOIT TRAIL

STEPS

TRAMPET

CRASH MAT

CLIMB ON TO HORSE

ROPE SWING

BOXES FOR STEPPING STONES

BENCH WALK

CLIMB ROPE LADDER TO HALF HEIGHT DESCEND OTHER SIDE

BOX TRAVERSE

HOOP TUNNEL

BENCH WALK

USING ADVENTURE PLAYGROUNDS

ropeway
or zip wire (consult 'Safety
in Outdoor Education')

ropeswing

totem poles

climbing nets

pipes and tunnels

stepped
posts or boxes for climbing

fallen trees or fences for
scrambling

ditches for jumping across or
crossing on balancing logs

ropes suspended over water
or ditch

KS: 2/3.
PoS: KS2: A and C; KS3: Unit A (a) and (b), Unit B (c).
Activity: walks and rambles (journeys into the countryside) A5.
Aim: to provide the opportunity to plan and prepare for a journey; to experience a journey through an unfamiliar area of countryside; to increase conservation awareness and an awareness of the nature of country life; to develop navigational skills with Ordnance Survey (O.S.) maps.
Time required: several theory-based classroom sessions of 30–50 minutes followed by a journey of between 3 and 8 hours.
Location: low-level land (below 600m above sea-level and not wilderness such as high mountain or moorland), open countryside, coastal (for example, South Downs Way), waymarked trails, forestry/country park trails, town pocket parks, national parks, national nature reserves, Sites of Special Scientific Interest (SSSIs), Areas of Outstanding Natural Beauty (AONBs).
Equipment required: 1:50,000 O.S. maps of area (preferably laminated or contained in a clear plastic map case/plastic bag), leader's kit (*see* 'Planning a visit', pages 81–5).
Target group: 11–13 year olds (shorter, less demanding walks for the younger ones). See 'Planning a visit' for suggested pupil/staff ratios.

Teacher's guidance notes

A journey into an unfamiliar, stimulating environment is deemed to be a desirable aspect of the KS2/3 OAA PoS. To be successful, the journey requires careful planning and a well-defined purpose that the pupils are aware of.

For practical reasons, the journey will be best undertaken on foot. Other journeys on water – using canoes, for example – may be possible with small groups after further training; alternatively, larger vessels and qualified staff may be sought for journeys with larger groups (for example, a fleet of longboats could stimulate cross-curricular links with History by investigating the origins of the longboat, Viking voyages, etc.).

Trips in winter conditions require extra precautions, although they do have the benefit of providing opportunities to see changes in vegetation.

The journey can provide a means of exploring a new environment, providing the pupils with a sense of discovery and an awareness of man's heritage of exploration and discovery (a well-documented aspect of our evolution which again could initiate a cross-curricular link with History – for example, Scott of the Antarctic). The journey also provides an opportunity to learn about the environment in which the activity is taking place (for example, coniferous forest plantations, fauna and flora, topography and physical relief, erosion, pollution, conservation of natural habitats). Preliminary training in the country code and in hill, coastal and seashore safety (if applicable) will instil a disciplined, respectful approach to the landscape ventured into.

(1) Preliminary planning:

(a) *see* pages 81–5 on planning a visit

(b) determine the aims of the journey and the cross-curricular input that is required, if any (for example, Home Economics – nutritional needs; Geography – the work of rivers)

(c) pupil training through the supplied resources in:

- walking skills and country code
- basic map reading skills (pupils will gain more from the journey if they can relate the map to their own position, and small groups can take turns to lead the party)
- climatic effects on the body (wet, cold, heat, sun)
- clothing and personal equipment
- elementary route planning
- other safety considerations appropriate to the activity.

(2) Other considerations:

- prevailing weather – a shorter, less demanding alternative route should be devised for bad weather
- length of the journey – 2–5 miles plus possibly a total of 300–400 metres of climbing should be considered
- choice of venue – is it stimulating, will it fit the needs of the trip, how long will it take to transport the group to the start point, is overnight accommodation required?
- how much time is required for the walk? – *see* pages 81–5
- group size – large groups will be slow, more difficult to control and harder to keep together, so more staff will be required
- cliff-top walks must be monitored more closely, especially in wet or windy weather – *see* pages 81–5

(3) Leader training and qualifications: there are two qualifications available in Great Britain for supervising walking parties: the MLTB Mountain Leader Scheme and the CCPR Basic Expedition Training Award (*see* page 95 for addresses). The former is aimed principally at those whose aspirations lie in leading groups over high moorland or mountainous 'wilderness' areas. It requires a big commitment, it is time consuming and therefore not really appropriate for this type of activity. The BETA award is closer to the mark and requires from the leader common sense, good map reading, and first aid and emergency skills (*see* pages 81–5).

I would, however, suggest that a formal First Aid qualification, administered by the St. John/St. Andrew/Red Cross organisations be obtained (*see* page 95).

Assessment: by direct observation, worksheets.

Cross-curricular links: Environment; Science; Technology; History; Geography.

Pupil resources: none. (It has not been practicable to reproduce detailed information on map work. This is widely available in Geography textbooks.)

JOURNEYS INTO THE COUNTRYSIDE

A journey into the countryside can be very enjoyable, especially if you live in a town or city. You will get the chance to see just how beautiful natural areas can be, and possibly see wildlife in its natural surroundings. You may be lucky enough to visit a National Park.

A National Park is an area of land that has been recognised as being of outstanding natural beauty with spectacular natural formations such as waterfalls, lakes and mountains. There are special rules regarding the use of the land to make sure that it does not get spoiled. We call this type of protection **conservation**.

Look at the map below. How many National Parks are there in England and Wales? Find out which one is nearest to where you live – mark your home on the map. Also, find out about Scotland's Scenic Heritage Areas.
What are Ireland's special areas known as?

NATIONAL PARKS OF ENGLAND AND WALES

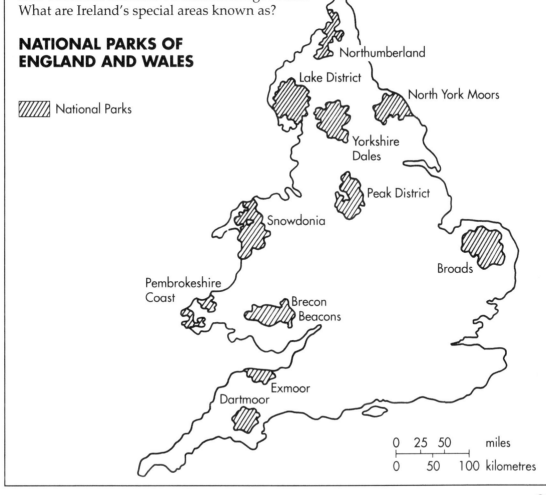

National Parks

Northumberland

Lake District

North York Moors

Yorkshire Dales

Peak District

Snowdonia

Broads

Pembrokeshire Coast

Brecon Beacons

Exmoor

Dartmoor

| 0 | 25 | 50 | | miles |
| 0 | | 50 | 100 | kilometres |

You may visit a Country Park (a sort of mini National Park), or a forest, or follow the route of a waymarked trail. All land in this country – even the National Parks – is privately owned, some by the National Trust (a charity which purchases areas of land for the public to use), and some by the Forestry Commission (which provides trails for visitors to follow through the forest and for people who work on the land such as farmers).

Whenever we go on to private land we should make sure that we are following a Public Right of Way. This might be a footpath, a bridleway (for horses as well) or a byway. All of these are shown on the maps you will be using.

If you are visiting the area for the first time, then your journey becomes more of an exploration into the unknown, like the journeys made by famous explorers such as Scott of the Antarctic. Can you think of any more?

On a separate piece of paper, draw a picture to illustrate each of the points in the Country Code. These are listed below.

- Go carefully on country roads.

- Respect the life of the countryside.

- Tread lightly to reduce footpath erosion.

- Don't pick flowers; take a photograph or make a drawing instead.

- Don't climb over and damage stone walls or fences.

- Fasten all gates.

- Keep dogs under control.

- Keep to paths across farmland.

- Don't leave litter.

- Don't contaminate water supplies.

- Protect wildlife, plants and trees.

KS: 2/3.
PoS: KS2: C; KS3: Unit A (b), Unit B (c).
Activity: effects of cold, heat, rain, snow and wind (C1).
Aim: to show pupils how the elements can threaten one's well-being; to emphasise the need for a conservation-minded attitude to life; to reduce pollution and halt ozone depletion.

Time required: three sessions of 30–50 minutes.
Location: classroom and school playing fields.
Equipment required: two mercury thermometers per group, colouring pencils and paper, pens.
Target group: 10–12 year olds. A class of 30, divided into groups of four for wind-chill experiment no. 2.

Teacher's guidance notes

Ideally this information is best delivered as part of a preparation programme for a journey into the countryside. A knowledge of the effects of climatic conditions on the body is most important for anybody who ventures out of doors to pursue challenging activities. By learning how to keep warm and dry in bad weather, or cool and free from the harmful effects of the sun in hot weather, the pupil will not only be able to enjoy activities more but will also be less likely to fall ill.

If any of the wind-chill experiments are undertaken, make sure that you choose a windy day and contrasting locations for the thermometer experiments.

The colouring exercise and instructional diagram graphics task will hopefully reinforce any teacher-led examination of the photocopiable material.

In looking at this section we can introduce the concept of conservation and increase environmental awareness by illustrating how man is destroying the planet through over-indulgence and exploitation. The issues of deforestation, the build-up of greenhouse gases and ozone layer depletion can be easily linked to this area of study. This in turn can lead into discussions on conservation measures such as planting more trees and grasslands, using smaller cars and unleaded fuel, sharing transport, using ozone-friendly products, and finding out about conservation bodies such as Greenpeace, Friends of the Earth, the Countryside Commission and the National Trust.

Assessment: by examination of pupils' classwork and experiment results.
Cross-curricular links: Environment; Health and Fitness.
Pupil resources: *see* worksheets.

Name _____

If you get ...

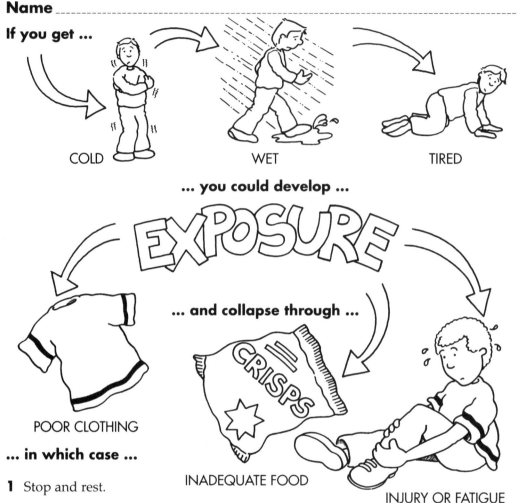

COLD   WET   TIRED

... you could develop ...

EXPOSURE

... and collapse through ...

POOR CLOTHING

... in which case ...

INADEQUATE FOOD

INJURY OR FATIGUE

1 Stop and rest.

2 Put on spare clothing.

3 Eat sugary foods and make hot drinks.

4 Shelter from wind and rain. Climb into a bivouac bag. Find an old building or a wall. Erect a tent or make a shelter if you can.

5 Try to summon help with distress signals. If possible, send two fit persons to dial 999.

Draw a set of pictures to illustrate your actions to deal with exposure.

HOT WEATHER AND THE SUN

Too much sun can cause you to collapse with fatigue and dehydration.

The emissions from car exhaust pipes, smoke and the cutting down of trees in the equatorial rain forests is creating what is known as the 'Greenhouse Effect'. More and more carbon dioxide in the atmosphere is causing the planet to heat up.

How can we reduce the Greenhouse Effect?

Prevention of heat disorders in hot weather

1 Keep fit.

2 Conserve energy; don't overdo it.

3 Drink and rest at regular intervals.

4 Keep out of the sun as much as possible.

5 Good quality food of a high nutritional value can help.

6 Wear loose, well-ventilated clothing, sunglasses and a sun hat.

7 The ozone layer protects us from harmful UVA rays from the sun. The ozone layer has been reduced by CFCs from aerosol cans. You can help to preserve the ozone layer by using ozone friendly products.

8 To protect us from UVB rays (which can cause sunburn) and UVA rays (which can cause skin cancers and cataracts of the eye), we must use a suncream. The higher the factor number, the greater the level of protection.

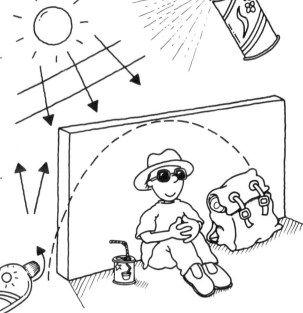

Label this drawing with the numbers of the points listed above. If you have time, use colours to show each point more clearly.

The next time you go shopping, try to find out what is the highest factor suncream on the supermarket shelves.

WIND CHILL

When the speed of air increases, its pressure decreases; this in turn causes cooling. Strong winds will have a marked effect on the temperature in exposed locations, for example a mountain ridge.

Try these other wind chill experiments.

1 Assess the windproofing of your clothing by blowing through the garment. Can you feel the air coming through the other side?

Now choose a windy spot on the school field. Put your best windproof garment on, then take it off again after a few minutes. Notice any differences?

2 Equipment required: two mercury thermometers. Choose a windy day to measure the temperature on the school field in the following locations: (a) the centre spot of the field (a = ?°C); (b) the edge of the field bounded by a wall or fence and so protected from the wind (b = ?°C). Note the difference between the two temperatures and determine the wind chill factor.

WIND CHILL FACTOR = $\dfrac{b-a}{b}$ x 100%

THE LAPSE RATE

In general, as you increase your height above sea level (for example, climbing a mountain), the temperature will decrease by about 3°C per 300m. Therefore, if the valley temperature was 3°C and you were going to climb a 300m hill, the temperature at the summit would be at freezing point. On a windy day, the summit temperature will probably be lower still! Rain in the valley may be falling as snow on the summit.

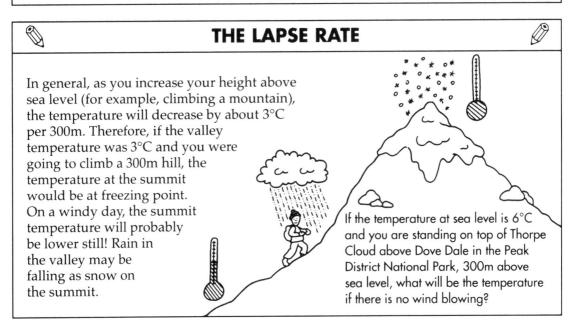

If the temperature at sea level is 6°C and you are standing on top of Thorpe Cloud above Dove Dale in the Peak District National Park, 300m above sea level, what will be the temperature if there is no wind blowing?

KS: 2/3.
PoS: KS2: C; KS3: Unit A (b), Unit B (c).
Activity: electrical storms (C1).
Aim: to educate pupils in how to minimise the risk of being struck by lightning during thunderstorms.

Time required: 20–25 minutes.
Location: classroom.
Equipment required: pens.
Target group: 10–12 year olds, a class of 30.

Teacher's guidance notes

A useful learning exercise which can be completed in class as an academic exercise. Explain that very few people get struck by lightning.

Once again, this work may be included in the preparation for a journey into the countryside. However, it is a good idea for children to know what to do if caught in a storm as a matter of course. Also, by learning a little about how lightning and thunder are formed we may help to reduce the fear associated with these awesome natural phenomena.

Pupils are required to digest the text and to relate the information given to the graphics. Pose the question: 'What is an electrical storm?' Try to lead pupils into realising that lightning is a powerful surge of electricity created by hot and cold air currents clashing and generating an electrical charge. The lightning conducts its way to the earth by 'hopping a ride' on droplets of rain (as water conducts electricity). It looks for the easiest way to earth via tall buildings, etc. Further discussion could lead to the need to 'earth' electrical appliances to prevent discharge through your body, electrical conductors on tall buildings and the need to insulate with rubber and plastic. Perhaps you could explain the dangers of using electrical equipment near water, such as in the bath or outside when it is raining.

Explain that thunder is the sound of the electricity rushing through the air, rather like a supersonic jet crashing through the sound barrier. You could also explain why you see the flash of lightning several seconds before the clap of thunder – i.e. because of the different speeds of light and sound. A useful follow-up activity is to take the group out on to the school fields and position a pupil at the furthest point possible from the rest of the group with a pair of cymbals. Get him to hold them up and crash them together once; there will be a delay before the sound reaches you.

Finally, explain that if you are with someone who gets struck by lightning they will probably need resuscitating and treating for severe burns. This could lead the group nicely into activity C1 (general safety).

Assessment: examination of pupils' answers on the worksheet.
Cross-curricular links: Science.
Pupil resources: *see* worksheet.

Name

Electrical storms can be dangerous; they can kill. Lightning is attracted to high and prominent ground such as mountains, trees and towers.

- If you are on an exposed ridge, carefully move off to a lower terrain.

- On no account shelter from the storm under trees, by walls or in rock cavities and land projections.

- Try to find some dry rocks on a shallow slope at the base of a hollow.

- Insulate yourself by standing or sitting on a survival bag, rope or rucksack. Avoid bodily contact with the ground - crouch or sit with the feet brought up to the chest.

- Wet ropes will act like electrical wires because the water will conduct the electricity.

- Early warning signs of an approaching storm: hair raising as a result of static electricity; metal objects humming; rumbling noises in the distance.

Look at the points above. Draw a lightning symbol at each place on the illustration below where you would expect lightning to strike. Put a circle around the correct place to be.

Remember, lightning will always try to find the easiest, shortest route to earth.

KS: 2/3.
PoS: KS2: C; KS3: Unit A (b), Unit B (c).
Activity: rivers (C1).
Aim: to increase the pupils' awareness of the dangers of moving water and to demonstrate safe methods of crossing.
Time required: 30–50 minutes.
Location: school playing fields for training, followed up with an actual crossing whilst on a journey.

Equipment required: stepping stones, tree stumps or upturned containers capable of withstanding the weight of a pupil, flags or pegs to mark the course of the river, measuring tape.
Target group: 10–12 year olds; a class of 30 in groups of 3, 6 and 1.

Teacher's guidance notes

As before, this activity could form part of a preparation programme for a journey into the countryside. Emphasise that crossing any river is a risky business and should only be undertaken under the supervision of your teachers. These techniques should only be practised in very shallow water – perhaps up to knee height – where there is no danger of being swept away by the current. For deeper, fast flowing water a safety rope is needed. In such cases the crossing should only be carried out as an emergency procedure when no other alternative is available, not as an activity in its own right. *See* pages 86–91 for more information.

Practise the techniques shown on the school playing fields, using cones or flag markers to describe the route of an imaginary river. Indicate the direction of flow, the position of a weir, an overhanging tree, and rocks in the middle of the stream creating eddies. Design a river that includes a large bend, a shallow and a narrowing. The pupils will have to decide which is the safest place to cross.

Further 'downstream' you can arrange a line of stepping stones across the river and explain that the pupils must recross the river using the stones. Anyone 'falling in' has to start again. Make sure that the stones are not too far apart for the pupils.

Demonstrate how easy it is to knock someone over if they are facing downstream by pushing a basketball into the back of a pupil's knee (but take care!).

If during an off-site visit the opportunity to do a river crossing does present itself, then it is well worth doing. Always make a crossing yourself first to ascertain the suitability of the water (on a safety rope if you are in any doubt as to the strength of flow and depth).

Assessment: examination of the pupils' answers on the worksheet and observation in the field.
Cross-curricular links: Geography.
Pupil resources: *see* worksheet.

Name --

We may be required to cross a river on our journeys into the countryside. Rivers in upland areas often run fast and can be very dangerous in times of heavy rainfall. Only cross rivers in flood if there is no other alternative, and only then with a safety rope. Your teacher will know how to do this if it becomes necessary.

- When do we cross? No bridge; long detour to bridge; darkness coming soon.

- Where do we cross? Current slowest; even bottom; shallow; no obstructions (e.g. overhanging trees); after a bend in the river; stepping stones.

- Where shouldn't we cross? Above waterfalls or weirs; bends; deep water; uneven bottom; in front of obstructions.

Put a tick where you feel it is safe and a cross where it is not safe to cross.

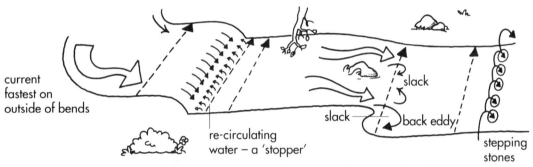

current fastest on outside of bends

re-circulating water – a 'stopper'

slack

slack

back eddy

stepping stones

- Precautions: slacken rucksack straps; take off socks; roll up or take off trousers; always face upstream and ferry glide across.

- Stepping stones: stay balanced; wet rocks are slippery; look ahead.

- Crossing methods (only to be attempted in shallow water):

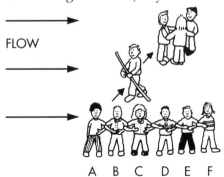

FLOW

A B C D E F

Three persons linking arms

One person with stick for support. Practise crossing stepping stones and these techniques in your school field.

'A' moves one space, then 'B', then 'C', then 'D', etc.

Perhaps your teacher may find a place where you can practise these methods.

KS: 2/3.
PoS: KS2: C; KS3: Unit A (b), Unit B (c).
Activity: emergency action (C1).
Aim: to acquire a knowledge of life-saving skills and of how to deal with an emergency.
Time required: approximately two sessions of 50 minutes.

Location: classroom.
Equipment required: 'Resuscitation Annie', triangular bandages, softwood splints (150mm + 10mm + 500mm), a selection of plasters, sterile dressings.
Target group: 10–12 year olds. A class of 30 in groups of two.

Teacher's guidance notes

One might argue that this core of knowledge and skill acquisition is the most important to learn in life, and yet how often is such training left to chance or completely ignored?

The best teaching strategies involve examination of the material in stages, interspersed with demonstrations by the teacher leading the activity and immediately followed by pupil participation. On no account let any pupil blow into the mouth of another when practising mouth-to-mouth resuscitation – demonstrate how to blow *over* the other side of the face. Points to emphasise are neck extension, loosening restrictive clothing, looking in the mouth for obstructions, looking for the rise and fall of the chest, action for vomiting, rate of inflation and recovery position. Resuscitation dolls are useful for practising cardiac compressions – **never let pupils practise this procedure on one another** as you can actually cause a cardiac arrest in this way.

It can be useful to contact the local First Aid organisation, which will be only too pleased to help you with any programme of First Aid you may be planning. The supervising teacher should hold a valid First Aid certificate themselves for legal purposes. Resuscitation dolls may be loaned out from the First Aid organisations; the PE adviser should also be able to help in this area.

Contact the Royal Life Saving Society (RLSS) for the crib cards; they are free of charge. I feel that every child should possess one.

Points to note with the shoulder sling are that the fingers should protrude and that the knot (a reef knot) should be at the shoulder. For leg splints, look for bandages placed either side of the site of the fracture.

Assessment: by direct observation.
Cross-curricular links: Health and Fitness; Citizenship.
Pupil resources: *see* worksheets.

Everybody should know how to deal with emergencies. You may be able to save somebody's life, possibly that of a friend or relative.

- Remove the victim from immediate danger if necessary. Summon help if required.
- Carry out any First Aid that is required in the following order of priority: AIRWAY, BREATHING, CIRCULATION (ABC); bleeding, fractures, shock, other injuries.
- Study the Royal Life Saving Society Emergency First Aid Card that your teacher has given you. Split up into pairs and have a go after your teacher has gone through the technique with you. **It is very important that you do not actually blow into your partner's mouth (blow over the far side of their head) or try to push down on their chest.** To be safe, you should practise on a dummy (a 'resuscitation Annie').
- Bleeding from cuts or wounds: remove any foreign bodies (glass, stones, etc.) and clean the wound with water or antiseptic. In the case of large wounds, slow down the flow of blood by pressing down with a pad (a sterile dressing) and bandaging firmly. Get medical help as soon as possible. With small wounds, clean as above, then apply a small plaster.
- Fractures, sprains and strains: do not move anyone who complains of neck or back pain, or of loss of feeling. Injuries to the arms can be immobilised with a sling (e.g. a triangular bandage).
- Injuries to the leg can be immobilised using a splint (e.g. a piece of wood) and bandages (not directly over the fracture). A sprained ankle may just need a cold compress to reduce swelling, and then bandaging.

Get medical help as soon as possible.
Now try to make an arm sling and leg splint for your partner; then swop roles.

- Shock: anyone who has had an accident will be in shock. They will complain of feeling sick and faint. Lay them down before they fall down!; then reassure them and keep them warm. **Do not give any accident victim anything to eat or drink.**
- Burns: immerse in cold water, cover with a wet cloth and seek help.
- Insect stings: pluck out any barb that may be protruding, apply insect bite cream if you have any to hand, and seek help.
- Dog bites: clean the wound, arrest any bleeding and seek help.
- Snake bites: the only poisonous snake in Britain is the adder. It has a V-shaped pattern on its head. It will only bite if threatened. If someone is bitten, try to wash out the venom with water and get the victim to medical help as soon as possible. The poison can be life-threatening in some cases.
- Protect all casualties by keeping them warm, dry and sheltered from the wind. If possible put spare, dry clothing on the victim before placing them in a sleeping bag (if available) and bivouac bag. Extra protection can be gained by placing the legs into a rucksack. **Remember: do not give drinks or food to anyone who is suffering from internal injuries or who may require an operation.**
- Reassure the victim if they are conscious. **Remember: do not attempt to move casualties suffering from neck or back injuries.**

Name _____

What should I do if I get lost or separated from the rest of the group? Stay in one place and try to attract attention by:

- Using the International Alpine Rescue Code (six shouts, whistles or torch flashes per minute followed by a minute's pause - a rescue party will acknowledge with three per minute).

- Shouting! Some of your class will be very good at this!

- Waving an orange or red article in the air (e.g. a plastic survival bag).

Plastic Survival Bag
Could also be used to
shelter from wind and rain

Put your spare clothing on and try to keep warm. Shelter from the wind and rain. Tuck into your emergency food. Keep signalling for help.

Can you think of another distress signal? Make a drawing of your answer in the space below.

What are the hazards I should be prepared for?

- Electrical storms.
- Rivers.
- Cold, wet, windy weather.
- Exposure.
- Wind chill.
- Hot, dry weather and heat exhaustion.

Name ....

What should we wear for our journey into the countryside?

On our feet? A pair of training shoes or Wellington boots is a good idea, especially if they have a good tread pattern and ankle support (it is very easy to twist your ankle on rough country paths). However, if you have a pair of fabric or leather walking boots, then this would be even better.

Does your footwear have:

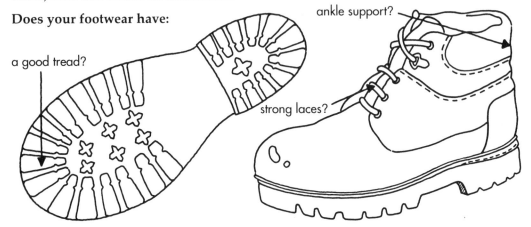

Leather boots can be waterproofed to some extent by rubbing a waterproof compound (available from outdoor shops) into the leather. Sprays can be bought for fabric boots.

Beware of new boots: they can be very painful and create blisters very quickly. Blisters are no joke when you are on a walk! Wear your boots around town for a few weeks and find out where the sore points are. If you start to feel your boots rubbing, stop and tighten the laces before a blister develops. If your feet start to feel sore, stop and put a plaster on the area of discomfort. If you do develop a blister, make the plaster into a ring pad to relieve the pressure. Do not prick blisters.

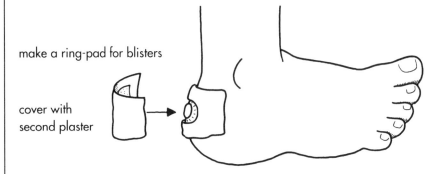

make a ring-pad for blisters

cover with
second plaster

Name --

What should we wear on our bodies?

We have to be prepared for bad weather. This means trying to keep dry and warm by wearing clothing that will keep out the wind, rain and snow and insulate us from the cold. In hot, fine weather we will want to stay cool.

The outer shell. We can keep the wind, rain and snow out by wearing an outer layer known as a 'shell' (not a shell suit!). A jacket that has a 'proofing' is required; the proofing makes the jacket waterproof.

We may get wet inside from sweat trapped inside the shell when we are working hard - walking uphill, for instance – but this is much better than getting chilled by an icy blast of wind or saturated by a downpour! Really keen outdoor adventurists wear waterproofs that can 'breathe'. However, these are very expensive and not necessary for our ventures.

Things to look for in waterproofs:

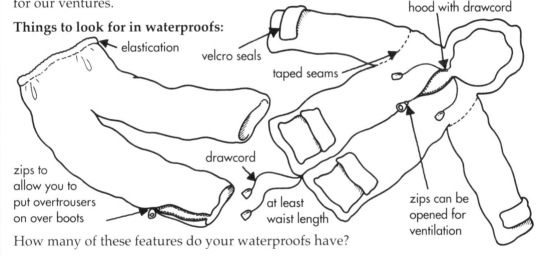

How many of these features do your waterproofs have?

Waterproof trousers are useful for the legs as well, but don't worry too much about this. It is your upper body that needs the most protection to prevent you from becoming a victim of exposure.

Tracksuit trousers, jogging bottoms or a pair of trousers that dry out quickly when wet and are reasonably windproof (remember the wind chill experiments?) are sufficient protection for your legs. In cold weather you could wear some pyjama bottoms underneath for added warmth, or you may own some long johns.

In summer, a pair of shorts can be worn underneath your trousers. Avoid jeans if you can – they offer no warmth when wet and take a very long time to dry out.

Name _____

Inside the 'shell'

The shell only needs to be worn in wet, windy conditions. Inside the shell we need to have a number of layers so that we can regulate our body temperatures according to how hard we are working and how much heat we are generating. This is how the layers work –

Where is the most heat escaping?

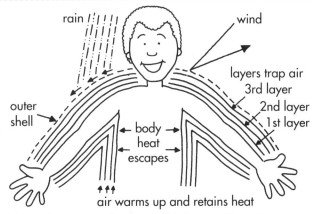

Several thin layers will be more flexible and warmer than one thick one. Here is a suggested 'layering' set-up for your walk –

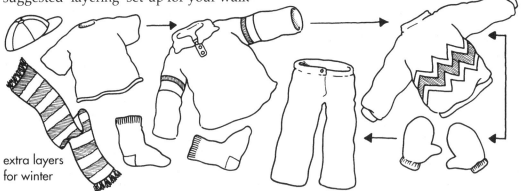

extra layers for winter

In winter you should increase your layers. The best layering materials are fleecy sweaters and jackets or woollens. These garments are very warm for their weight (even when wet!) and dry out very quickly. Ski anoraks (which are normally windproof), sweat shirts, rugby shirts and T-shirts can all be used for our walk.

What about my head, feet and hands? These areas of your body lose heat quicker than anywhere else. On all walks it is wise to have a pair of gloves and a ski-style hat or balaclava. A scarf may also be useful. Wear a pair of thick socks if you have them; failing that a pair of football socks and a pair of thin socks may be the answer. Try to keep your feet dry; wet, cold feet are very unpleasant. In summer, it will be necessary to protect your head from the sun with a baseball cap or some other form of sun hat.

On a separate piece of paper, make up checklists for clothing required on journeys from April to October, and from November to March.

Name ....

What else should we take with us?

- A spare layer such as a ski anorak, fleece jacket, sweat shirt or sweater for rest stops and emergencies.
- A packed lunch (sandwiches, crisps, chocolate bar, nuts and raisins, biscuits, apple, orange). Food should be convenient to carry and have a high carbohydrate content (e.g. sugar) for energy.
- A sugar-based drink for energy. Hot drinks in vacuum flasks will be welcome in wintry weather. Cans of fizzy drink are not really suitable unless you intend sharing – drink little and often is the best policy, and once you open a can you have to drink all of it! Keeping fluid levels up is very important; you must replace fluid lost by sweating in order to prevent dehydration.
- Food for emergencies (not to be taken unless your teacher tells you to or you are desperate!). This could be a king-sized bar of chocolate, or Kendal mint cake which can be bought from any outdoor shop.
- A reliable torch, spare batteries and a spare bulb in case our walk finishes in the dark. Walking in the dark can be very exciting!
- A whistle to attract attention if you get lost, but please no whistling as we go along. We are here to enjoy the peace and quiet.
- A small, personal First Aid kit.
- Your teacher will provide each group with an Ordnance Survey map of the area and possibly a plastic survival bag if the route takes you on to high ground.
- A small rucksack, big enough to hold all the items you need to carry. Make sure that you either wrap up all the items you need to carry in plastic bags or line the sack with a large plastic bag (e.g. a dustbin liner).

See if you can identify and label the items above in the drawings below. (On some walks your teacher may decide that some of these items are not needed.)

YOU PROVIDE   TEACHER PROVIDES

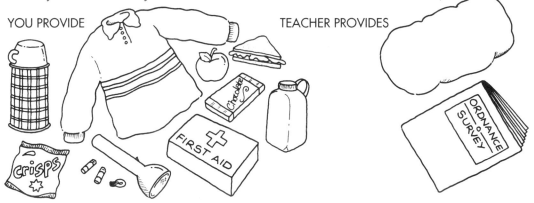

Name --

What other skills do I need to learn?

Complete the information below by making your own 'cartoon' drawings on a separate piece of paper to illustrate the points more clearly.

A Types of terrain

1 Grassy slopes. Nice to walk on because the grass has a cushioning effect, but – 'Whoops!' – they can be very slippery when wet!

2 Heather moorland. Heather is a shrub-like plant. Tread carefully.

3 Peat bogs – 'Yuk!'. Messy and tiring to trek through.

4 Scree. These are slopes of pebbles and larger stones which are very tiring to climb but can be exciting to descend (don't go too fast). Dig your heels in and don't lean forwards.

5 Rough, rocky paths can cause you to stumble and fall. They have been formed by the thousands of pairs of feet that have tramped over them, eroding the topsoil. Footpath erosion is a conservation problem in some areas such as the National Parks. Wardens and volunteers are constantly carrying out restoration work - like the roadworks on the motorways! If the path is steep, use your hands to support yourself. Remember that the rock itself can vary in texture from smooth sedimentary rock such as limestone, to coarse volcanic rock such as granite. (Your teacher may have a number of rock samples to show you in class.) Rocks are very slippery when wet.

B Walking skills

1 We must always keep together to prevent someone getting lost. We should go at the pace of the slowest. It is not a race: let's try to encourage those who may not be as athletic as others.

2 We must try to develop a steady, rhythmic pace. It is foolish to rush off at break-neck speed, because you will become tired very quickly. On steep slopes, you will have to shorten your stride, walk at a slower pace than normal, and rest more often.

3 Have you ever noticed how most very steep paths and roads up mountains zig-zag up and down, or gradually climb at a lesser angle around the hillside? You will find that ascending and descending slopes in this way will be far less tiring than attacking the 'fall line' direct. Ask your teacher what is meant by the 'fall line'.

4 We will try to set ourselves targets to reach before we stop for a rest. See them as little challenges – places which offer a good view and shelter from wind and rain.

5 We will probably have one or two food stops to break up the journey and keep our energy levels up. Don't eat all of your lunch at the first stop!

6 Use your clothing wisely; put on extra layers when you stop for a break. Don't climb hills with excessive clothing on, because you will overheat and sweat rapidly.

7 Most accidents occur towards the end of a day, normally when descending. Try to concentrate and look where you are going at all times.

Name _____

1 We are going to observe one minute's silence when instructed to do so by your teacher. In the space below, write down every noise you hear.

How do these noises differ from noises in the town or city?
If you were able to do the same experiment in your town or city before you came on the journey, compare your two lists.

2 As you travel through the countryside on your journey, observe the following and write down any differences (numbers, type, size, shape, etc.) compared with similar features in the town or city.

a Rivers and streams _____

b Lakes _____

c The shape of the land ('topography') _____

d Vegetation on the ground _____

e Trees _____

f Soil _____

g Animals and birds _____

h Flowers _____

i Fences and walls _____

J Houses/dwellings _____

k Paths _____

l Motor vehicles _____

m People _____

n Roads _____

Ask your teacher if you do not understand any of these questions.

Name _____

Your teacher may be able to arrange a visit to an orienteering event or a permanent orienteering course. The venue will probably be a forest.

Permanent orienteering courses have been set up in lots of forests, heathlands, country parks and moorlands. Throughout the United Kingdom, most are supervised by the Forestry Commission or local authorities. Specially prepared maps are usually available from a warden's office of the offices of those directly responsible for the course.

Orienteering courses normally take the form of red and white painted posts or boards bearing an identification mark – if you are in a competition – or a piece of equipment designed to leave a symbol on your route card.

Competitive orienteering is a popular sport. Teams or individuals race against each other, hoping to find all the markers and complete the course in the shortest possible time. Failure to locate a marker incurs time penalty points which are added on to your finishing time.

There are many competitions organised throughout the country each year for all levels of ability. If you would like to find out more about the sport of orienteering, ask your teacher for the address of The British Orienteering Federation.

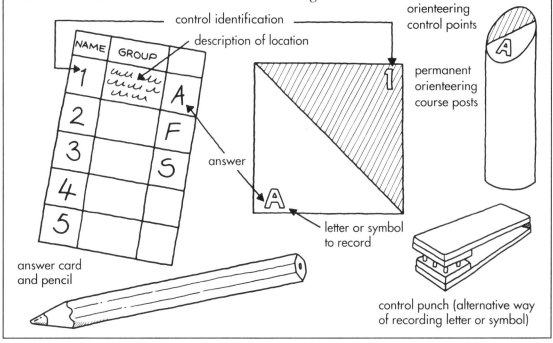

answer card and pencil

control identification

description of location

answer

letter or symbol to record

orienteering control points

permanent orienteering course posts

control punch (alternative way of recording letter or symbol)

Name ....

The navigating compass

The model shown in the drawing below is the most common form of navigating compass used for orienteering and has all the features necessary for the compass navigation you will be doing with your teacher.

When carrying out any compass navigation techniques, always make sure that the RED (North) end of the compass needle aligns with the orienting arrow in the compass housing.

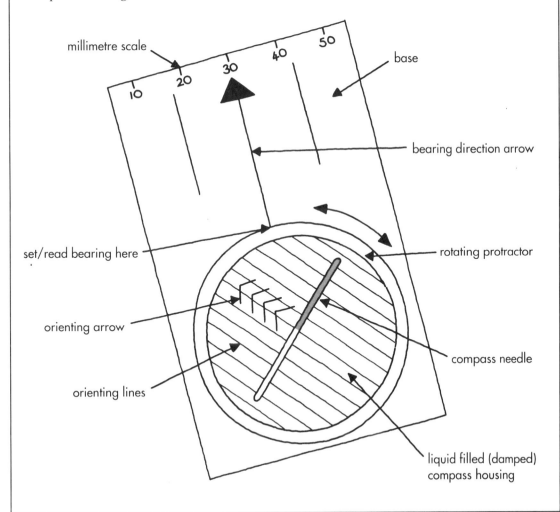

millimetre scale

base

bearing direction arrow

set/read bearing here

rotating protractor

orienting arrow

compass needle

orienting lines

liquid filled (damped) compass housing

Name --

Orienteering skills

Pacing techniques

Pacing can help you determine distances when moving around the course.
The average person takes 60 double paces per 100 metres.

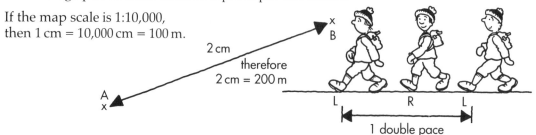

If the map scale is 1:10,000,
then 1 cm = 10,000 cm = 100 m.

2 cm

therefore
2 cm = 200 m

1 double pace

If 160 double paces are used (i.e. count one foot
movement only) then the rate is 80 per 100 m.

On a steep slope, the orienteer finds that his pacing goes up to 120 per 100 m.
How many paces must he take when AB = 4 cm and the slope is steep?

Answer ----------------------------

An orienteer will work out his or her personal pacing for level, uphill and
downhill terrain.

Exercise

Now try some pacing techniques on your school field.

a Select a known distance between two features in the field on fairly level ground.
Count the number of double paces taken to cover this distance. Repeat this several
times, walking back and forth to find the average. Work out the number of paces
per 100 m. This is your personal pacing rate for level ground.

b Now repeat the experiment for a steep slope of known distance.

PERSONAL PACING RECORD

NAME: --

PACING FOR LEVEL GROUND: --

PACING FOR STEEP SLOPES: --

Name ....

Orienteering skills

Setting the map
This technique will help you to decide which way to go. To set the map, draw imaginary lines from yourself to features on the map. Turn the map until your imaginary line points to the feature.

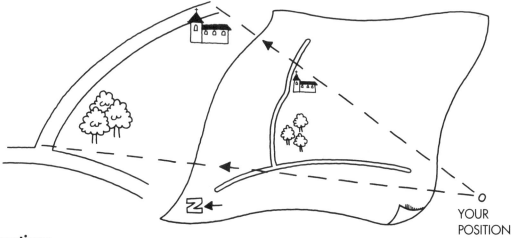

YOUR
POSITION

Junctions
Always stop at junctions in paths and set your map to make sure that you know in which direction to continue.

Thumbing
This involves keeping your thumb on your present position. You will be able to save valuable minutes in this way every time you need to consult the map.

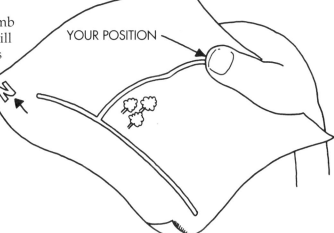

YOUR POSITION

Name --

Orienteering skills

Working out your route

Take note of the nature of the terrain between checkpoints. Avoid the 'fight' shown on the map below – it is always a fight to get through! Going in a straight line may not always be the quickest route.

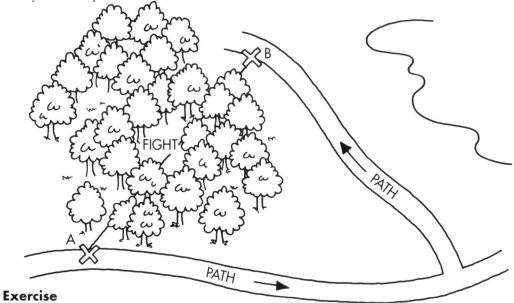

Exercise

Your teacher will provide you with an orienteering map of your school field or local area. Use the skills you now have to complete the course.

Notes

1 There will be a 10-minute penalty for each missed or incorrect answer.

2 Stay together. Your group time is calculated on the last member of your group returning.

3 Take extra care near any water.

4 Don't climb bridges or go on to roads.

5 Use paths.

6 Use the Green Cross Code on routes in built-up areas.

Name _____

Orienteering techniques

Compass techniques

To set a bearing of 20°:

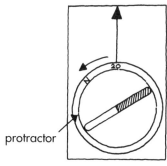

protractor

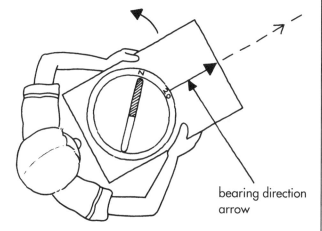

bearing direction arrow

a rotate protractor until 20° is at the top

b rotate yourself and the compass on the spot until the RED (North) end of the compass needle lines up with the 'N'. Look along the bearing direction arrow.

Important – Keep away from metal objects because they will affect the magnetic needle. See what happens when you move your compass close to a chair or table with metal legs.

Exercise

Now go out on to your school field and take the bearings listed by your teacher at the specified locations (e.g. athletics shed – 40°). Write down the landmark you see on the bearing at each checkpoint.

GROUP NAMES: _____

LOCATION	BEARING	LANDMARK

Name _____

Exercise

Go to the location specified by your teacher and take the first bearing listed. Walk the specified number of paces on this bearing and take the second bearing and so on until you have completed the course. Leave a coloured marker at each checkpoint.

Where have you ended up? Can you name the shape formed by your markers?

Collect them up and move on to the next station when your teacher tells you to. Move clockwise around the course.

Walk _____ paces on each bearing.

LOCATION 1: 8 markers
Bearings:

  90°
135°
180°
225°
270°
315°
360°
  45°

Shape? _____

LOCATION 2: 4 markers
Bearings:

  90°
180°
270°
360°

Shape? _____

LOCATION 3: 6 markers
Bearings:

  90°
120°
210°
270°
330°
  30°

Shape? _____

LOCATION 4: 3 markers
Bearings:

120°
270°
  60°

Shape? _____

GROUP NAMES:

Name ---

Exercise – compass bearing orienteering

Look at the map provided by your teacher. You must visit checkpoints A to E in turn in a clockwise direction around the school field.

At each checkpoint you must take the bearings listed below, locate the object on the bearing, and write down the answer in the space provided.

Accuracy is important.

CHECKPOINT	BEARING	LANDMARK	BEARING	LANDMARK
A				
B				
C				
D				
E				

Exercise – compass bearings and pacing trail

Complete the trail, writing down the name of the locations at the end of each leg of the trail.

Remember
- 1 pace = counting when only left or right leg comes forwards, e.g. L-R-L = 2 paces.
- Beware of roads - keep to the path.
- Each member of your group takes turns at each stage of the trail.

START:

LEG	BEARING	PACES	LOCATION

GROUP NAMES:

KS: 2/3.
PoS: KS2: A6 and C3; KS3: Unit A (a) and (b), Unit B (c) and (d).
Activity: residential experience – camping and bivouacking.
Aim: to promote teamwork and tolerance of others, and to provide a vehicle for residential experience. To develop campcraft skills.
Time required: one night (minimum).

Location: static camps on approved camp-sites or school field; bivouac sites close to human habitation in coastal/woodland environments.
Equipment required: tents, stoves, fuel, bivouac materials ranging from plastic survival bags to poles, rope, polythene sheets, large stones.
Target group: 11–12 year olds. Groups of up to 30.

Teacher's guidance notes

Note A teacher wishing to embark on this type of activity should possess all the relevant campcraft skills. Numerous textbooks are available.

Camping is an extremely rewarding activity for promoting personal and social development – a highly effective form of residential experience. Children regard camping as an adventure, an opportunity for them to live out of doors.

A previous residential experience using a youth hostel or similar location may be advisable, as this will form a good introduction to residential experience before tackling the more demanding routines required in camping.

The camping trip may serve as a means of pursuing other activities such as day/night walks, orienteering or night lines. A night line is a rope line which is threaded through a forest for a distance of a 100m or so; the pupils have to follow the line on their own. Care must be taken to ensure that pupils cannot sustain eye damage – for instance, do not select a route which winds through densely overgrown vegetation.

Make sure also that a member of staff is at the other end and possibly post another hidden helper somewhere along the route.

Startling children with spooky noises and movements is not to be recommended as it could have a detrimental effect. Attaching the rope(s) to trees with slings and climbing karabenas can help to maintain rope tension (tie off the rope at each karabena with a figure-of-eight knot).

Successful bivouacs and camps rely on good planning and preparation – not to mention good weather. Bivouacking is a good way of providing this type of experience when tents are not available or when a more adventurous outing is sought. Some local educational authorities operate a loan service: enquire via your PE adviser.

• This form of residential experience should be confined to between April and October. Remember that days are short in April and October and frosty nights can be very cold under canvas.

• Consult the DFE's 'Safety in Outdoor Education', your local LEA's codes of practice, and HMSO's 'Camping' for further guidance.

- Adhere to the advice given in the section 'Planning a visit' (pages 81–4), especially regarding the close supervision of girls, pupil/staff ratios, staff gender for mixed groups and sanitary arrangements on sites with no facilities.
- Ensure that all pupils have warm, waterproof clothing and all other items specified on the kit list.
- For camps where the cooking is done on a communal basis, make sure the pupils know the routine for meals and chores. No activities should commence until all chores are completed. For camps where the children cook for themselves, each tent should operate as a separate unit.

- Pre-visit training in campcraft skills as detailed in the pupil resources is essential.
- Make sure that you have booked and visited the site before the visit.
- Instil safety awareness regarding the dangers of cooking, contamination of food and fuel leakage.
- Tents must be hung to dry back at base.
- The staff must be aware of accident procedures and at least one member should be qualified in First Aid.
- Obtain an up-to-date weather forecast, be prepared to abandon the activity or to seek better shelter if hostile weather is forecast.

Assessment: by direct observation in the field and by examination of responses to pupil resource material.

Cross-curricular links: Environment; Health and Fitness; Citizenship.

Pupil resources: *see* worksheets.

Name --

Food for the camp

- Your teacher may have decided that he or she will bring all the food for the group. If so, you will be informed of the menu.
- Are you a vegetarian? Do you have to have a special diet? If so, see your teacher and explain in good time for special arrangements to be made for you.
- If you are cooking your own food, you must decide on a common menu with the rest of your tent group, and decide who is going to bring what. Bear in mind what it's like trying to prepare food out of doors on a small camping stove. Your meals should be simple to prepare all at once in one pan (e.g. stew).
- You do not need to bring any special dehydrated meals that are quite expensive to buy in outdoor shops. Tinned foods, pot noodles, packet soups, etc. will do fine because we don't have to worry about the weight in the same way as we would do if we were carrying the food and camping equipment on an expedition.
- Don't forget your tin opener, scouring pad, washing-up liquid and matches.
- Keep milk and other fresh food out of the sun.
- Try to bring food that will provide a high level of nutrition (protein) and energy (carbohydrate) to make up for the extra demands put on you during the activities.
- All foods have a 'calorific value'; this is a measure of the energy they can provide in the form of sugar or fat. Cereals and fruit will help your digestion.
- The following foods are high in nutritional value and will provide you with a high-energy, balanced diet.

meat stew · soup · chocolate · pasta · tea bags · SOYA MEAL · cheese · beans · MARG · salt · vegetables · COFFEE · crisps · bread · rice · dessert · nuts · cereal · sugar · raisins · sultanas · milk · dried fruit · potatoes

Name --

Cooking skills

Your teacher may have decided that there will be a 'cook tent' where all food is prepared by the staff and/or a group of pupils for the whole group. If, however, you are cooking for yourselves, you need to learn how to use a small camping stove. (Your teacher may ask you to bring one into school if you have your own.)

Remember that the flames from the burner can be very dangerous, especially those from pressure stoves and from stoves that use petrol. For our safety you will only be allowed to use stoves that use gas cartridges or methylated spirit fuel.

Your teacher will demonstrate and check that you know how to use your stove.

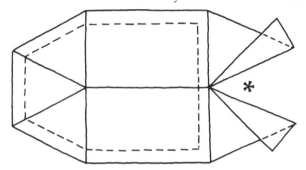

On no account cook inside the main tent. In bad weather, bring the stove inside the flysheet. But beware of flare-ups!

Rules

1 The stove must be in the mouth of the tent, as shown in the drawing above*.
2 There mustn't be any spilt or spare fuel nearby.
3 Only one person must cook; everyone else must sit still.
4 Fill stoves outside the tent.
5 Make sure that the fuel bottle and stove caps are secure.

Exercise

Equipment required: camping stove and pan, clean water, teabags or coffee, milk, sugar, scouring pad, water container.

When your teacher has shown you how to use the stove, boil a pan of water and use it to make a cup of tea or coffee. When you have finished, clean up all your equipment with the scouring pad.

Name _____

Campcraft skills

- Each tent or bivouac group should operate as a separate unit.
- Only take those items on the equipment list.
- Take a spare set of clothes in a plastic bag. (This can also act as a pillow.)
- Be settled in your tent or bivouac shelter and finish any cooking by nightfall if possible.
- Hang wet tents to dry back at base to prevent rotting.
- Always wash your hands before handling food, especially after visits to the loo or after handling fuel.
- An insulation mat or airbed under your sleeping bag will keep you warmer and is more comfortable than sleeping on the ground.
- Always sleep head-to-tail in small tents where there isn't much space.

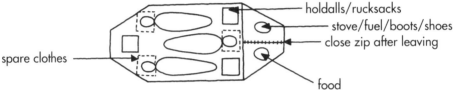

- Keep all rubbish in a dustbin or plastic carrier bags.

Living in the tent in bad weather

The important point here is to reduce movement to a minimum.
- Remove boots before placing feet on groundsheet.
- Remove waterproofs outside; store them in a corner of the tent or underneath the flysheet.
- Before settling down to cook, make sure that you have all you need, e.g. water for both cooking and washing up.
- Try to keep the inside of the tent neat and organised.
- In cold weather, stuff as much clothing and as many plastic bags, etc. as possible underneath your sleeping bag to insulate you from the cold ground.

Hazards

- Tents are covered with inflammable material: don't have named flames inside or close to the tent.
- Never leave gas cylinders in the tent: a layer of toxic gas may build up overnight and suffocate you.
- Always cook outside: bring the stove into the front of the tent in foul weather.

LEAVE THE SITE CLEAN AND TIDY!

CAMPING AND BIVOUACKING

Name --

- Camping and bivouacking are great ways of living out of doors. They can be a lot of fun and a really memorable adventure, especially in the countryside at night.
- A bivouac is a shelter which will protect you from the wind and rain.
- We will have a better time if we learn how to keep ourselves warm, dry and comfortable, and make sure that our camping and bivouacking equipment is in good order before we leave the school. Our camp or bivouac activity will take place during the summer months – winter camping calls for more specialised equipment to keep you warm.
- Some outdoor adventurers like to carry their camping equipment with them on their journey, and possibly camp in wild, remote places. This is known as 'backpacking'. You may get the chance to make an expedition like this when you are older and stronger.
- We can use our camp as a base for other activities such as night lines, orienteering, and day or night hikes.
- We should always get permission from the camp site owner before we attempt to set up our tents or prepare a bivouac site. Approved camp sites will have clean water for drinking and cooking, toilets and washing facilities. Remember also that sound carries a long way out of doors, so try to be settled and quiet between 11pm and 7am.
- Camping and bivouacking in the wilds can be a great adventure, but again we must get permission first from the landowner and choose a site where we can get fresh water. The water should be crystal clear and free from any mud or smell. Clean water is difficult to find other than in the mountains, and even then it must be boiled or treated with purification tablets (which you can buy from chemists). It may be possible for your teacher to take the water with you in a large drum with a tap.
- If you are camping in the wilds you must also make your own arrangements for toilets, washing up and washing. Someone in the group must be prepared to dig a trench 150 cm deep for people to use to go to the toilet. Waste is covered as necessary with a trowel.

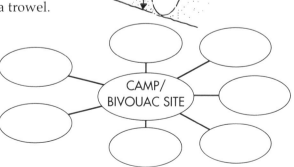

150 cm

What makes a good camp site?
Fill in and colour the spider chart with things that you feel make a good camp or bivouac site.

Now share these ideas with your teacher and the rest of the group. Extend the spider chart if necessary to add your teacher's answers.

CAMP/ BIVOUAC SITE

Name _____

- To build a bivouac we need to use many of the skills we have learnt for camping. However, we must now ask ourselves: How can we shelter from the wind and rain?

- A bivouac bag – normally a man-size, orange-coloured plastic bag – makes an acceptable shelter. Mountaineers carry one for emergency use. However, you do tend to end up quite wet from condensation.

- Complete the spider chart below by inserting as many solutions as you can think of to the problem of providing shelter.

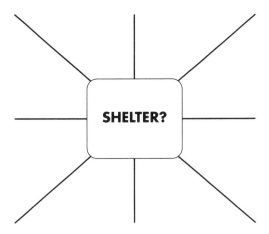

SHELTER?

- Now let's go out on to the school field and prepare a bivouac shelter with the materials provided by your teacher.

KS: 2.
PoS: A7 and C4.
Activity: visits to the seaside.
Aim: to increase awareness of the coastal environment and marine ecosystems.
Time required: preferably 3–8 hours.
Location: coastal areas protected by the National Trust, country parks and coastal footpaths, ideally away from seaside resorts. Coastline should be easily accessible and offer opportunities to explore rock pools, mussel beds, etc. There should be no dangerous currents or places where the incoming tide may cut off pupils and sweep them out to sea. Steeply shelving beaches with dangerous undertows must also be avoided. *See* pages 86–91.
Equipment required: marine organism identification sheets, graph paper, clipboards, quadrats, transect lines.
Target group: 10–11 year olds.

Teacher's guidance notes

The dangers of school children undertaking activities on coastlines were highlighted by the Land's End tragedy. Choose your day and location carefully (*see* pages 86–91).

Everyone enjoys a visit to the seaside, especially pupils who live some distance away inland. It can be a stimulating experience, particularly if the coastline is relatively remote and rugged.

Preliminary classroom work relating to the seashore environment and the seashore code, and visits to the seaside should be undertaken prior to the visit.

There are a number of physical activities one can pursue, such as exploring caves, follow-the-leader and scrambling (*see* pages 86–91), in addition to less active sessions such as scavenger hunts, cooking freshly caught fish (purchased earlier from fishermen) and beach transects. Other activities might include a visit to a local 'sea life centre'.

(1) Scavenger hunt. The tide must be at low water. Pupils are given a well-defined area, visible by the staff from a suitable vantage point, and an identification sheet. They are asked to bring back a specimen of each species detailed. On a simple outline plan of the area they can mark where they found the specimen. By comparing plans it may be possible for pupils to work out that different specimens live at different parts of the inter-tidal cycle.

(2) Transect. Pupils are given a blank profile for each location, a quadrat (a measuring square) and a transect line. Specimens are counted and plotted on the graphs for each square metre along the line from low water to high.

Assessment: physical activities: direct observation. Environmental activities: worksheets, graphs.
Cross-curricular links: Science; Environment; Conservation; Geography.
Pupil resources: *see* worksheets.

Name _____

- The seashore can be a great place to have fun and adventure. Your teacher may be able to arrange a visit to undertake a marine scavenger hunt, trail quiz or coastal walk.

- Coastal walks, along the top of cliffs or along beaches, can involve exploring coves and caves, scrambling over large rocks or traversing at the base of cliffs, and can be very exciting.

- What else could we do? We might try cooking over an open fire or even spending the night on the beach or in a cave. This is known as 'bivouacking'.

- We must respect the power of the sea and be wary of the dangers that can be present at the seashore.

- The sea rises up the beach and falls away again every six hours to create a 'tide'. The highest point the water reaches is known as 'high water'.

What is the lowest point known as? _____

The tide is biggest when there is a full moon and smallest when the moon is at half phase.

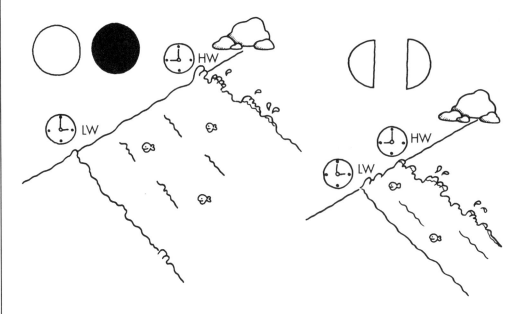

- The wind causes the waves that crash against the beach.

MARINE LIFE IDENTIFICATION CHART

Name _____

GROUP 1

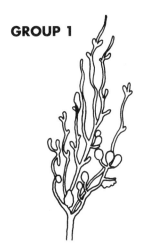

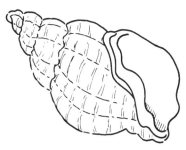

COMMON PERIWINKLE
(full size, black or beige)

COMMON WHELK
(full size, look for underside slit)

EGG WRACK
(% cover per m² transect)

GROUP 2

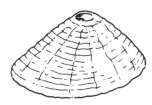

LIMPET
(beige, conical shell)

ROUGH PERIWINKLE
(full size, red to black, look for
horizontal ridges on shell)

FLAT WRACK
(% cover)

GROUP 3

BARNACLE
(% cover)

FLAT PERIWINKLE
(full size, variable colour –
yellow, orange, green)

CHANNEL WRACK
(% cover)

Name ....

Blank profile – exposed beach GROUP .... TIME .... DATE ....

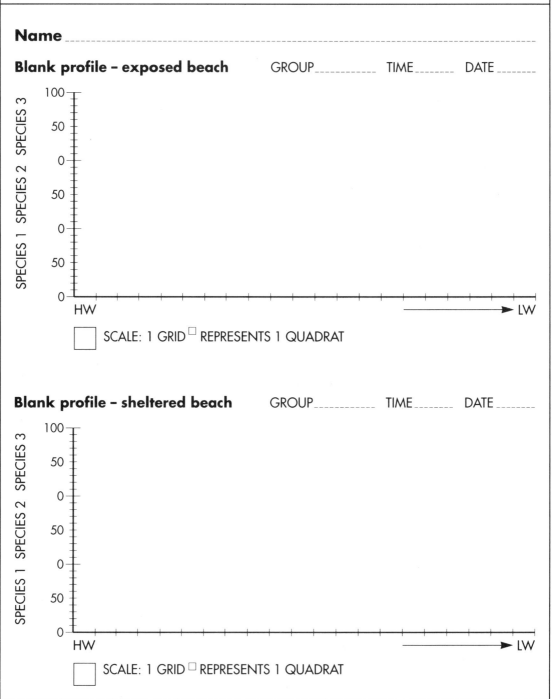

SPECIES 1 SPECIES 2 SPECIES 3

100 50 0 50 0 50 0

HW → LW

SCALE: 1 GRID ☐ REPRESENTS 1 QUADRAT

Blank profile – sheltered beach GROUP .... TIME .... DATE ....

SPECIES 1 SPECIES 2 SPECIES 3

100 50 0 50 0 50 0

HW → LW

SCALE: 1 GRID ☐ REPRESENTS 1 QUADRAT

Name _____

Study with your teacher the safety points listed below. Fill in the missing blanks and create an information poster by making drawings on a separate piece of paper to illustrate the safety rules. The first one has been done for you.

■ Don't ignore warning signs.

■ Beware of becoming stranded by incoming tides. If caught, try to climb above the high water mark. Beware of going into caves that might flood.

■ Don't go in or on the water in windy weather. Why? _____

_____

■ Don't swim if a red flag is flying. Only swim on beaches patrolled by lifeguards.

■ Red and yellow flags mean that lifeguards are on patrol and that it is safe to swim.

Name --

- Don't swim near pipes, rocks, piers or breakwaters. Pipes that lead into the sea often carry sewage and industrial waste. Pollution of the sea has become a worrying problem and a number of surfers and regular bathers have suffered with intestine infections. Clean beaches are given an award – look for the flag below.

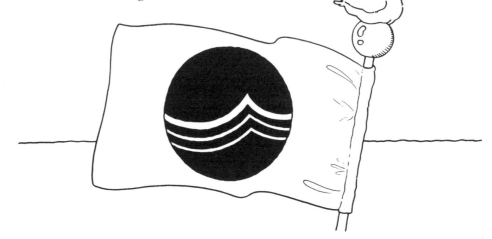

Can you think of other ways in which the marine environment is being polluted?

How do you think this might be affecting the creatures that live in the sea and people like fishermen who earn their living from the sea?

Seawatch is a conservation body that is dedicated to protecting the marine and coastal environment. They have a number of Sea Life Centres where you can see the creatures of the sea close up. Your teacher may be able to arrange a visit to one for you.

- Make sure that you know what's beneath the surface. Why? ----------------------

----

- Learn how to help someone in touble. Learn basic lifesaving and rescue skills. Ring 999 and ask for the coastguard in an emergency.

- Don't let yourself get too cold in the water. You may get cramp or hypothermia. Wear a wetsuit if you are going to be in the water for a long time (e.g. surfing, snorkelling).

Name _____

- Don't swim after a big meal.

- Beware of 'rip currents'. These are strong currents that can carry you out to sea. If you are caught in a rip, try to swim parallel to the shore until you are clear of it.

- Always swim parallel to the shore.

- Don't take lilos and inflatables on to the sea when the tide is going out, near rip currents, or when the wind is blowing offshore.
  What does 'blowing offshore' mean? _____

  _____

- Keep well clear of boats.

- Beware of sitting under cliffs. The rocks above may be loose.

- On some beaches there can be strong undertows. Only go into the sea from beaches that are gently sloping or are approved for water activities. Never go out in rough conditions.

- Beware of going too close to the edge of cliffs. Keep to paths and well away from cliff edges, especially in wet, windy conditions. Watch out for gusts of wind that could carry you over the edge.

- Don't try to climb up or down cliffs unless you are with an experienced rock climber. Scrambling along the base of cliffs or over large rocks on the beach (under the supervision of your teacher) can be great fun as long as you don't climb too high. Wear a helmet. Make sure that the rocks are not loose and that you are not going to be cut off by the tide. 'Coasteering' is an exciting adventure activity which combines climbing skills with swimming and jumping into the sea; however, you need to wear a buoyancy aid or lifejacket and a wetsuit. You must be properly supervised for your own safety.

KS: 2/3.

PoS: KS2: B; KS3: Unit B (d).

Activity: problem-solving activities.

Aim: to share ideas and work together on specified problems of a physical nature; to develop teamwork.

Time required: each activity should start with a written brief of what is required of the group, followed by a 5–minute 'thinking time'. All the activities will run for about 30 minutes except raft building and rafting, which should be tackled in isolation over a period of 1–2 hours. The other activities can be arranged in a 'circus' system – over a two- or three-period session.

Location: in the school grounds; on a slow-moving river or lakeside.

Equipment required: *Centipede:* two planks, tape or rope slings. *Acid stream:* two planks, three acid-resistant pedestals (for example milk crates). *Square dance:* rope, blindfolds. *Dots and lines:* 9 quoits, rope. *Retrieving the bucket:* bucket, boundary rope, coils of rope long enough to span boundary, miscellaneous equipment not needed. *Reef knot around the tree:* rope. *Filling the leaking container:* large 'well' dustbin filled with water, leaking transporting swing bin, leaking dustbin to be filled. *Raft building and rafting on placid water:* plastic/steel drums, planks/poles, rope, paddles/oars, buoyancy aids/lifejackets, helmets, inner tubes/tyres/polystyrene blocks.

Target group: 11–13 year olds.

Teacher's guidance notes

Centipede

Pupil brief

You are to use the planks and slings provided to move your team over the specified distance in the shortest possible time. The whole group must move together in formation with both feet in contact with the planks at all times.

Solution/ teacher's notes

Acid stream

Pupil brief

Your group must cross the acid stream in the shortest possible time. The only acid-resistant equipment that you have are the three pedestals. If a member of the group falls into the stream, start again.

Solution/ teacher's notes

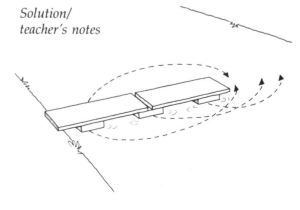

78

Slings used as handles to lift planks. Feet placed on each plank.

Square dance
Pupil brief

Assemble by the joined rope that has been laid out on the ground for you. Elect one member of your group to issue instructions. The remainder of the group then blindfold themselves. Only the leader may speak; he or she must get the rest of the group to form a square with the rope in the shortest possible time.

Any other member of the group attempting to use verbal communications will cause the group to have to start again.

Solution/teacher's notes

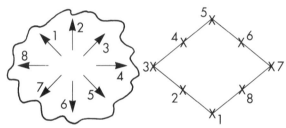

number group walk/crawl to rope on instructions of 'left, right, forward, back'

Dots and lines
Pupil brief

Using the rope provided, devise a means of joining all the quoits with four straight lines. You will be timed.

Solution/teacher's notes

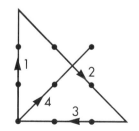

Retrieving the bucket
Pupil brief

Using any of the equipment provided, devise a method of removing the bucket from the centre of the boundary circle – without trespassing inside – in the shortest possible time. If any member trespasses the group must start again.

Solution/teacher's notes

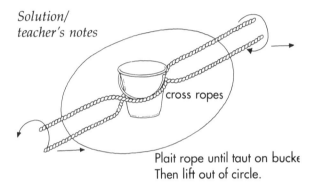

cross ropes

Plait rope until taut on bucket Then lift out of circle.

Reef knot around the tree
Pupil brief

Look at the diagram of the reef knot tied around the tree. A reef knot is tied by 'over-left, over-right', then 'right over left'. Your group must use the rope provided to tie the reef knot around the tree in the shortest possible time. The rope is covered with glue so that once you pick it up you must remain in contact with it. If any member of the team lets go the group has to start again.

Solution/teacher's notes

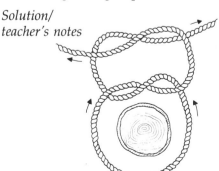

Filling the leaking container
Pupil brief
Your team must attempt to fill the leaking dustbin with water transported in the leaking bucket. You will be timed and the height of water achieved will be measured.

Solution/teacher's notes
When drilling holes in the carrying vessel, drill them in such a manner that outspread fingers could 'plug' the holes. Some members of the group may use their fingers to plug holes.

Raft building and rafting on placid water
Pupil brief
You are to build a raft and cross the expanse of water in front of you in the shortest possible time. You may use any of the materials provided. You must all wear a buoyancy aid/lifejacket and helmet before attempting to launch your craft.

Solution/teacher's notes
Raft building encourages the pupils to share their ideas and develop practical skills, improvising with given materials to create a seaworthy craft capable of crossing a stretch of placid water. The water must be placid, i.e. still or slow moving, for negotiating river currents and especially white-water – of any description – requires the use of specialised inflatable rafts and a qualified helmsman.

A brief discussion on paddling skills before the exercise begins is useful. Perhaps you could liken the movements to those of a fish's fins: for example, 'flick the left fin and the fish will move to the right'; the tail or dorsal fin (the helmsman) provides the steerage. The helmsman gives commands, such as 'left forward', 'right back', 'forward together', 'reverse together', etc. to manoeuvre the craft.

You could also describe: sitting/kneeling/standing positions on the raft; balancing and gripping the paddle; taking care with double-bladed canoe paddles not to hit people on the head; what to do if the raft becomes unseaworthy and the crew have to abandon ship. On small rivers where the bank is never too far away, pupils should swim on their back. On larger expanses of water, such as a lake, there should be a motorised power boat in attendance. Other factors such as surface drift and wind direction are significant.

Pupils could be given the task of getting from A to B using a set course (such as sailing markers). This activity is best reserved for the summer months to avoid any possibility of hypothermia through immersion in the water. Furthermore, I feel that this activity should only take place if a qualified RLSS lifesaver is in attendance.

An extension of this activity could include a visit to the white-water rafting centres in Bala, North Wales or in Nottingham.

Note A minimum swimming ability of 10m (50m on lakes) must be insisted upon.

Assessment: by direct observation.
Cross-curricular links: Technology.
Pupil resources: pupils need problem brief sheets adapted from text included above.

PLANNING A VISIT

Off-site visits for educational purposes are an accepted aspect of modern teaching. They are strategies for the reinforcement of subject matter studied in the classroom, a means of learning new skills and practising existing ones, of promoting PSME and experiencing new environments. A school visit creates a great deal of excitement among young children so that it can be used as a motivating force in the classroom. A visit will provide opportunities for implementing the process of physical education, namely:

PLANNING, PERFORMING EVALUATING

• **Planning:** pupils can be involved in choosing clothing, footwear and equipment, plotting routes on maps, bringing food and finding out about the areas to be visited.
• **Performing:** using the skills taught at school on-site.
• **Evaluating:** producing records and exhibitions; writing an account of activities.

At KS2 there is a pronounced emphasis on exploring new off-site environments. It may be possible for a visit to be made at KS1 (for example, to a local forest where the children can follow a short nature trail and possibly use adventure play areas for activity circuits). A school visit of any kind requires a lot of forethought and prior planning. Here is a list of factors to bear in mind when proposing an off-site experience for the pupils.

• Parents should be notified by formal letter with a reply slip and a medical consent form. The latter should ask for details of any medical condition that the supervising staff should know about, of any medication being taken and of the pupil's swimming ability. It should ask consent for emergency First Aid to be carried out if necessary. The telephone number of the family doctor, together with a contact telephone number and address, should also be obtained (*see* sample form on page 84, which may be photocopied if required).

The letter should outline the purpose of the trip, the cost, the planned activities, personal requirements regarding clothing, food, equipment and spending money, the departure time and meeting place and the estimated time of return (*see* sample letters on pages 83–4).

Regarding the cost of trips, legislation has deemed that if a visit takes place for the most part in curriculum time and is seen as part of the curriculum, then the school must fund the trip. Parents can be asked to provide voluntary contributions. If, however, the trip takes place for the large part in extra-curricular time (say at the weekend), then the cost of the trip must be borne by the pupils. The school may make an extra charge for the maintenance of equipment, staff INSET related to the activity, etc., but this must be clearly stated on the letter to the parents.

Always keep a record of all purchases with receipts. A balance sheet should be drawn up and submitted to the school Bursar after the trip. Do not forget that VAT is reclaimable for school trips.
• Always give pupils the opportunity to ring their parents when returning to school from a visit that has taken place in extra-

curricular time. This will let parents know when to come to collect their children. If there is equipment to be stowed or unpacked then make allowances for this. Do not leave any pupils unattended, especially after dark, once the trip is over. If you are likely to be delayed, ring as soon as it is convenient.

• At motorway service areas, rest stops, etc. ask pupils to keep in groups of four. Give specific times of return (30 minutes is normally sufficient), no-go areas and cautions about strangers. Make sure that pupils know where the vehicle is in relation to the car park as a whole. Warn pupils about moving traffic within service areas (I also warn my pupils about spending too much money). At what age you allow your pupils to go unsupervised is a difficult question that can only be answered according to individual situations. Finally, make sure the pupils know where you will be in an emergency.

• Long journeys can be very frustrating for children. I try to stop every couple of hours, preferably at a point where there is something interesting to look at or do (the French auto-route rest stops are well ahead of us in this respect). On extremely long journeys, an overnight stay will be required – an opportunity to make a standing camp, to bivouac, or find a youth hostel. I always look for accommodation that will not hinder the journey a great deal. Some skiing trips using coach travel require pupils to sleep through the night whilst travelling. Travelling through the night can itself be a big adventure for children.

Finally, on long journeys, always make generous allowances for travelling times. Rushing to meet deadlines is both dangerous and mentally exhausting. Gone are the days when motorway travel was fast and smooth!

• For any visit, consultation should first take place with the head teacher and possibly other staff. Visits requiring an overnight stay are classified as a residential visit, and some LEAs have a form which must be completed for such trips. However, with schools becoming more and more accountable for themselves, many schools are devising their own application forms.

• It may be wise to take out an insurance policy for the visit through the LEA insurers in order to cover the pupils for accidents, loss of personal belongings, liability, etc. Staff are covered for third party liability as employees of the authority, provided that they are acting with the consent of the head teacher and operating within accepted codes of practice. A copy of the LEA's code of practice for educational visits and outdoor pursuits should be available from your head teacher or PE adviser.

• Transporting a group has become quite complicated with the recent legislation relating to minibuses. In most cases your school's insurance will require you to have a clean licence and to be over 25 years of age in order to drive. The bus will need to carry a Bus Permit (available to all schools free of charge). The bus will have a log book which must be completed for every journey – a tedious business, but one which is essential if you are to remain within the law. Tachographs will soon be compulsory for Britain to fall in line with the rest of the EC. The minibus must have a side door for passenger access/egress, especially if a trailer is being towed. If you are driving abroad, in addition to a green card.(soon to be abolished) you need a waybill and model control document (available from the Bus and Coach Council in London). There are also recommendations relating to the availability of a portable telephone on minibus journeys of two or three hours. Consult your local authority for more details on this and also on towing a trailer.

• It is very important to observe recommended pupil/staff ratios, which for most visits will be 15:1. To have two members of staff is safer. For hazardous outdoor activities the ratios drop dramatically. Your codes of practice will provide guidance.

• Pupils should be fully briefed prior to the visit regarding what will constitute acceptable conduct and what will not. It can be useful to include this in the parents' letter. With younger children there are likely to be fewer problems than with, say, 11 year olds.

• A pre-visit by the supervising staff is highly recommended in order to rehearse the activity, seek out provision for toilets, lunch spots, parking, access, alternative bad weather activities/routes, etc. In the case of potentially hazardous outdoor pursuits, the implications for the supervising staff if an accident occurred and no pre-visit had been made are very grave.

• Always try to find out what the weather is going to be like and change your plans to suit. For example, it is no good trying to introduce canoeing to a novice group on a river in flood. The weather may have a marked effect on the safety of the activity: rocks become slippery to climb in the wet, and strong winds can sap one's strength.

• Leader's skills.
(a) Always appoint another member of staff to bring up the rear and keep the group together. There should be regular 'head counts'. Large groups should be sub-divided into smaller groups with a member of staff for each group.
(b) At least one member of staff should be a qualified first aider through the St. John Ambulance or a similar organisation. I have included a section on emergency First Aid under the supervision and safety section of the book (*see* pages 46 and 86–91).
(c) Understand what to do in an emergency and how to effect improvised evacuations. Again I have included these skills in the supervision and safety section.
(d) Have a good practical knowledge of navigation techniques.

• Extra considerations for residential trips.
(a) For mixed residentials it is recommended that there is a male member of staff for boys, a female member of staff for girls.
(b) Extra supervision is required for young pupils and girls.
(c) There may need to be a member of staff responsible for management of pupils' spending money. Records should be kept in these cases.
(d) What provision is being made for the evenings? Organised activities or free time?
(e) Will the children be allowed to go unsupervised off-site? At what times? Under what conditions? Where may they go and what may they do?
(f) If the residential is camp-based, then it should take place between the months of April and October – bearing in mind that spring and autumn days are short, and the nights long and cold!

Sample consent form

Activity leader ....   **Pupil's name** ....

School address ....   **Address** ....

.... **tel** .... **tel** ....

Activity ....   **Dates** ....

Dear Mr Balazik

1 I hereby give consent for my son / daughter to attend adventure-based outdoor activities organised on behalf of the school.

2 I understand that these activities have inherent 'potential' dangers and, whilst the staff in charge of the party will take all reasonable care of the children, the staff cannot necessarily be held responsible for any loss, damage or injury suffered by my son / daughter arising during or out of the school journey; unless the staff are found to be negligent in their duties.

3 I accept the extent of the personal insurance arrangements made by or on behalf of the leaders of this activity, to cover the party for expenses for medical requirements and unavoidable cancellation, and insurance for personal accident, personal effects and third party. Note: further details of the policies may be obtained from the activity leader.

4 National Health Service   **Doctor's name** ....

                                Doctor's tel ....

5 I certify that my son / daughter is / is not subject to:
- heart disease
- respiratory disease
- epilepsy
- asthma
- any other complaint or allergies (please state) ....

6 My son / daughter is / is not required to take drugs. I will ensure he / she takes an adequate supply. (Please state drug, times of dose, reason for taking drugs.)

....

7 I consent to any emergency medical treatment necessary in the case of illness / accident during the course of the activities.

8 Can your son / daughter swim 50m in light clothing? (This is a pre-requisite for acceptance on water-based activities.) YES / NO

Signed (Parent / guardian) .... Date ....

Sample letter

Dear parent/guardian

WHITEWATER KAYAKING: date of trip ----------------------------------

I shall be organising a whitewater kayaking trip to the river Derwent at Matlock, Derbyshire. The cost is £10.00 to cover the cost of minibus hire, staff training and maintenance of equipment.

We shall be leaving the school at 9.00am and hopefully returning at about 7.00pm. This trip is not suited to beginners (BCU 2 Star is the minimum standard). Previous experience of kayaking on flat water is essential. Your son/daughter must be able to swim. If in doubt, please contact me.

Your son/daughter will need to bring a change of clothes, towel, lunch and drink. The following is required for the kayaking: training shoes, thermal/cotton T-shirt, warm socks/wetsuit boots, sweatshirt or fleece garment, and a wetsuit if available. There should be an opportunity to visit other facilities at the watersports centre during the day.

I must know if your son/daughter suffers from heart disease, asthma, epilepsy or any other complaint that may be aggravated by immersion in cold water. Please note that if your son/daughter becomes unwell following immersion in river water, you should contact your doctor. There is the very remote chance of catching Weil's Disease which has been known to be fatal if left untreated.

Please return the slip below, together with payment and the attached medical consent form.

Yours sincerely

D. Balazik AD.DIP.O.ED.
Head of Outdoor Pursuits
BCU Senior Kayak Instructor (E1)

Name of student

I wish my son/daughter to take part in the whitewater kayaking trip. I enclose a cheque for £10.00 made payable to Sponne School.

Signed -- (parent/guardian)

In promoting an outdoor adventure activity the supervising teachers must accept that they are ultimately responsible for the safety and welfare of the pupils. If an outside agency is taking responsibility for the activity then to some extent the level of accountability is diminished, but it may be argued that the contracting of the outside agency has been the responsibility of the teacher organising the activity on behalf of the school and its pupils. Further advice and information on the latter is given on pages 92–3.

I would always advise teachers to work strictly within the guidelines set by your LEA and those stated in the DFE's 'Safety in Outdoor Education' to ensure that a claim of negligence would be difficult to uphold in the event of a mishap.

In the case of hazardous outdoor pursuits (climbing, abseiling, zip wires and ariel ropeways, canoeing, sail-based activities, mountain-based activities, air-based activities, sub-aqua, etc.), the LEA has a duty to ensure that adequate INSET programmes are available where required or to acknowledge national qualifications and experience. Some LEAs operate a log-book accreditation scheme for teachers wishing to introduce these activities at a 'taster' level. The national qualifications are really aimed at those individuals who are in an overall position of responsibility or who are seeking professional, vocational status in this area of educational experience. National qualifications for the most part assume previous experience and personal competence, and are expensive and time consuming. Teachers who are suitably trained and working within the codes of practice will be covered by the LEA for third party claims of negligence.

General points regarding safety

(1) Supervising staff should take steps to acquaint themselves fully with potential risk situations involved in a particular activity, and to devise approved strategies to combat the danger. These may include:
(a) eliminating the risk by changing or modifying your plans
(b) reducing the risk by increasing the supervision
(c) using appropriate safety equipment that is in good order (climbing equipment in particular requires close scrutiny and maintenance). Contact the relevant governing body for the sport for further advice. Addresses from the Sports Council
(d) psychological/physical support.
(2) Try to make sure that any venture you organise is flexible and carefully structured. Do not leave things to chance! Ensure that the activity has been 'rehearsed' at the designated venue where practicable.
(3) You should always operate in such a way that you yourself are confident in any situations that the activity may present.
(4) You should be aware of and well practised in emergency procedures.
(5) Has the activity been pitched at the correct mental/physical level for the group?
(6) Is the group too large?
(7) Is there an escape plan?
(8) Where close supervision is not possible, such as during orienteering in a forested area, then the pupils require briefing in an emergency plan. For example, in the event of an accident, leave one person with the

casualty, keep them warm, send two people to base or summon help with distress signals.

You should always be prepared to answer the following questions.

(**1**) Does the activity have a purpose and desirable educational aim?

(**2**) Am I fit emotionally/physically to lead this activity?

(**3**) Do I have the necessary technical skills and experience?

(**4**) Am I working within LEA guidelines and my qualifications/experience?

(**5**) Have the pupils been briefed in an accident plan where needed? Do I have the necessary First Aid kit/training to deal with any mishap?

(**6**) Do I know how to effect a rescue?

(**7**) Do the pupils have the physical/mental attributes to cope with the activity? Have they received adequate training?

(**8**) Have the parents completed a consent form and medical questionnaire? Is the approval of a doctor required for any of the pupils?

(**9**) Are the pupils aware of their own limitations and capabilities?

(**10**) Are the pupils equipped nutritionally and clothed adequately for the activity?

(**11**) Do the pupils have the correct personal equipment for the activity? Have they been trained in its usage?

(**12**) Do the pupils understand the purpose of the activity?

(**13**) Is the size of the group appropriate (consider the aims and nature of the activity, the need for communication, management, rescue and evacuation)?

(**14**) Are you familiar with the area to be visited and effects of bad weather on the nature of the terrain (for example, bad visibility on featureless moorland, heavy rainfall creating swollen rivers)?

(**15**) Is the venue sufficiently remote to create difficulties in getting to help in an emergency – where is the nearest telephone?

(**16**) Do you need to leave details of your activity with someone who can contact emergency services if required? N.B. Always remember to make contact on your safe return!

(**17**) Are you using public rights of way (PROW) for your activity; are you trespassing? Have you a legal right to access/egress on any water you may be using?

(**18**) Are you and the pupils aware of any conservation issues that are relevant to the activity (for example, country code, footpath erosion)?

(**19**) Are the pupils briefed as to any vital infections that may be contracted from activities involving water (for example Weils Disease)?

Supervision tips

(**1**) Be friendly but firm.

(**2**) Insist on quietness and on the pupils' full, undivided attention when giving instruction. At some off-site venues there are often distractions out of one's control: wait until they have passed, or choose a new spot for briefing.

(**3**) Keep the group together. Lead from the front. Do not let any pupil force the pace. I sometimes put the weakest member of the party at the front with me and let them set the pace, including rest stops. This gives the weaker ones more incentive.

(4) Address any negative comments by pupils immediately before they escalate. Do not tolerate chastisement of pupils by other pupils. Reprimand silly, irresponsible actions; threaten to terminate the pupils' involvement or to curtail the activity if it continues (this normally works if you have got the activity right!).

(5) Ensure that your assistant(s) are fully briefed. One should act as a 'tail-end Charlie' to keep the group together.

(6) By keeping your group together you will avoid losing members, and prevent exhaustion or disillusionment.

(7) When giving a demonstration or passing on instruction, make sure that the group can see and hear you. Don't take it for granted – ask them. Try to position yourself so that the sun is not in their eyes. On windy days try to position yourself upwind.

(8) Keep descriptions and demonstrations as brief as possible. Don't waffle on! Don't try to teach too much at once. There are a number of good instructional strategies in common use:

EDICT: Explanation, Demonstration, Imitation, Correction, Testing.
IDEAS: Introduction, Demonstration, Explanation, Activity, Summary.

A good maxim for all of us involved in communicating information might be:

KISS: Keep It Simple, Stupid!

(9) Make your demonstrations slow and deliberate. If you have ever watched a good ski instructor at work, you will notice how smooth and pronounced the actions are. Break down a procedure into progressive steps. Make sure the group can see clearly what you are doing – ask them: 'Can you see what I am doing?'

General safety skills and additional knowledge for supervisors of KSI and KS2 activities

For hazardous outdoor pursuits you will need to seek further training.

For off-site activities you will need a First Aid pack containing: sterile dressings, bandage, triangular bandage (2), antiseptic cream, scissors, antiseptic wipes, tape, paracetamol, salt tablets (for heat related conditions), high energy tablets, chocolate bars, Kendal mint cake (available from outdoor shops), antihistamine cream (for insect bites and stings), muscular rub (for strains and sprains).

In addition to the above, for activity A6 (camping and bivouacking) I would carry puritabs (available from chemists or outdoor shops) to purify water, and diocalm for upset stomachs.

For activity A5 (walks and rambles) I would also carry:

• a safety rope (30–45m). This could be a 7–9mm diameter hillwalker's safety rope or a 10/11mm climber's rope – heavier, but also useful for climbing. This could be used to construct an improvised evacuation stretcher, improvised carries, or to cross a river.

• a bivouac bag for treatment of hypothermia (a plastic survival bag is inexpensive and available from outdoor shops)

• an emergency stove for treatment of hypothermia. A small, portable affair that burns methylated spirit or camping gas is ideal

• a box of lifeboat waterproof matches

- a sugary powdered drink
- spare boot laces
- notepad for messages, a pencil and coins for telephone. All stored in plastic sandwich bags
- protractor-based navigating compass (basic model is adequate).

Precautions for coastal/ cliff walk activities

(1) Keep the group well away from the edge of cliffs, especially in windy weather. Gusts can be fatal!

(2) Instruct the children not to wander off on their own.

(3) Do not allow climbing of cliffs. However, climbing over large rocks or along the base of the cliffs can be very enjoyable. A word of caution here: ask yourself if the rocks above are loose, if there are any warning notices about climbing on the rocks, and if you are in danger of becoming cut off by the incoming tide.

(4) Note the weather forecast for the area, especially any warnings of strong winds or gales which will make the sea rough.

Keep the children well away from the water in rough conditions in case they are caught by a wave and swept out to sea. Rocky shores are particularly dangerous as the waves can rebound off the rocks. Sadly – as if one needed to be convinced of these dangers – one is reminded of the Land's End tragedy in which a group of school children were swept to their deaths whilst beachcombing in heavy seas. Harbour walls and exposed sea fronts or piers can present similar dangers.

Beaches can present other dangers such as undertows and rip tides (*see* 'The Sea-shore Safety Code', pages 75–7). If water-based activities are planned, such as swimming, snorkelling and canoeing, seek advice about the conditions and choose sheltered sites where help is at hand if needed. Ensure that you have the necessary training and experience to lead the activity, that the group is not extended beyond its abilities, that the equipment used is suited to the activity and that you and the group know what to do in an emergency. Do not underestimate the power of the sea; it can cause you to lose control of an activity with disastrous consequences If you are in any doubt about the conditions, contact the coastguard.

(5) Do not allow children to sit under the base of cliffs unless you are sure that there is no loose rock which may tumble down.

(6) 'Coasteering' is a relatively new form of coastal adventure activity whereby pupils are set numerous challenges involving abseiling, climbing, swimming and jumping in the sea from rocky platforms.

Qualified, experienced personnel with life saving abilities, a rescue boat and prior knowledge of the area are essential for this hazardous adventure activity. Pupils should be equipped with wet suits, buoyancy aids, climbing harnesses and helmets.

Heat exhaustion (hypothermia)

The effects of excessive heat can be quite devastating. Heat exhaustion is brought about by loss of body fluids and salts through profuse sweating. Victims are generally unaware of their condition.

If the condition has been brought on by water deficiency, the victim will complain of acute thirst, fatigue and giddiness. The pulse will be rapid and the victim will have a high temperature. Treat the victim by giving sips of water at first then as much as required.

If the condition has been brought on by salt deficiency, the victim will exhibit the above symptoms (but the temperature will be normal) and also complain of muscle cramp. Salt in the form of a salty drink or as tablets should be administered to restore the balance.

Heat stroke

This is a serious extension of heat exhaustion. The symptoms are very similar to those of hypothermia (slurred speech, aggression, poor vision, etc.). The skin appears very hot and dry (no sweating). Other symptoms may be observed as for heat exhaustion.

Treatment is as for heat exhaustion plus fanning and sponging with cold water. If possible, immerse the victim in cold water, but do this *gradually* otherwise the shock may be fatal.

Cold exhaustion (hypothermia)

This extremely dangerous condition is caused by a lowering of the body's core temperature. It is also known as *exposure*.

Causes: immersion in cold water, exposure to chilling wind and rain, inadequate clothing, fatigue, injury, lack of energy-giving food. Children and the elderly are more susceptible than others.

Signs and symptoms: impaired vision, shivering, difficulty in breathing, abnormal heart rate, slurred speech, irrational behaviour. Collapse and unconsciousness (a serious deterioration leading to death within hours) will result if the symptoms

are ignored. The casualty is often unaware of his condition.

Treatment: rest and keep warm. Offer warm sugary drinks if conscious, and reassure. Try to replace any wet clothes with spare dry clothing; place the victim in a sleeping bag if available and an emergency shelter such as a tent, plastic survival bag or any natural shelter available.

Consider exposure victims as invalids even if their condition improves. Do not rub the skin or give the patient alcohol as this will draw blood and body heat away from the inner core. Rapid re-warming should also be avoided. Immersion in a hot bath or shower is acceptable for victims with mild exposure. Severe cases of exposure should be evacuated to safety as soon as possible. Shock may develop in some casualties. Apply expired air resuscitation if breathing fails; external cardiac compression may be necessary in extreme cases.

Frostnip and frostbite

This condition is an indication that the central core is drawing on all its blood supply to conserve body temperature. It is the result of a lack of blood in constricted blood vessels due to low temperatures. Exposure can develop quite easily from here.

Frostnip and the progression to frostbite affects the extremities which offer the least resistance to chilling (nose, mouth, fingers, toes, ears). Frostbite can lead to the loss of limbs and death through gangrene.

Frostnip signs and symptoms: whiteness and numbness in the affected parts, localised pain.
Treatment: re-warm affected parts as quickly as possible on a warm part of the

body; put on insulated clothing or use the warmth from a fire.

Frostbite signs and symptoms: treatment for frostnip is ineffective. Frostbite results in immobility of affected parts, discoloration (blue or black), dead tissue and blisters.

Treatment: if re-warming is carried out it should be done rapidly and only if there is no chance of re-freezing occurring. In the field it is wise to immobilise the affected part, protect from further cooling and exposure before evacuating to base as quickly as possible.

When back at base, immerse the affected part in a hot bath for about 20 minutes or re-warm from indirect sources such as an electric fire. Do not prick blisters, do not rub the skin, do not give the victim alcohol and do not apply heat from solid objects.

Burns

Immerse the affected part in cold water if possible. Do not prick blisters. Apply a sterile dressing and treat for shock. Severe burns may reduce the body fluid levels; in these cases it may be advisable to give the casualty drinks to restore fluid levels. Finally, try to protect the affected area from further injury.

Sunburn

Move the victim into the shade and apply calamine lotion to the affected areas. Liquid intake will reduce dehydration.

Dislocations and sprains

Use a triangular bandage to immobilise the injured limb and evacuate to base. A cold compress is useful to reduce swelling. A crêpe bandage is useful for sprains.

Stings

Remove the sting and treat with antihistamine cream immediately.

Bites

Snake bite: The only poisonous snake in Great Britain is the adder. Unfortunately it is common in upland areas. Treat the victim for shock and attempt to draw out the venom from the wound by washing it and applying antiseptic. Seek immediate help and commence expired air resuscitation if necessary.

Dog bite: treat the bite as one would do for an ordinary wound. Seek medical assistance when possible to guard against rabies.

Seasickness

A common problem when kayaking on the sea is rough conditions! Raft up and comfort the victim, lower the head towards the front of the kayak. Get to solid ground as soon as possible. Travel sickness pills taken prior to the journey may be advisable for those prone to seasickness.

Cramp

This is a muscular spasm. Causes include overwork, loss of body salt due to excessive sweating, physical injury, cold.

Signs and symptoms: severe pain, loss of the use of the limb and mild shock.

Treatment: stretch the limb and rub vigorously to improve the circulation; treat for shock if necessary. It may be helpful to offer salt tablets.

You may decide to extend the pupils' range of experience by taking them to an 'external provider' – perhaps as a residential activity or for a one-off day visit. There are numerous private agencies such as country outdoor activity centres and dry ski slopes which are in the business of attracting schools to buy in their expertise and facilities. For a number of years, private centres have been able to operate without having to enforce the restrictions placed upon LEA-run centres which must comply fully with the Health and Safety Codes of Practice as detailed in DFE's 'Safety in Outdoor Education'. LEA centres have found it increasingly difficult to compete with commercially run centres whose prime purpose is after all to make a profit. There are some excellent private centres to be found, but some leave a great deal to be desired, employing inexperienced, underqualified staff and providing poorly structured programmes.

Inevitably, as LEAs and schools look to make savings, more and more business has flowed from the diminishing number of LEA centres to the private sector.

The lack of accountability and absence of a code of practice or regulation was sadly brought to light in 1993 when a number of children lost their lives during a canoeing accident at Lyme Bay. Following this tragedy, the government issued new legislation stating that it was the responsibility of schools to satisfy themselves as to the suitability of any agency that may be employed by the school. Furthermore, with the approval of the Secretary of State for Education, the English and Welsh tourist boards (who have their own form of accreditation) set up in conjunction with relevant national governing bodies and outdoor associations the Activity Centre Advisory Committee (ACAC).

In November 1993, following a report by the ACAC, the Secretary of State for Education announced a four-point plan to improve working practices in the private sector which will form the basis of a new code of practice:

• an immediate survey and inspection of all centres
• the publication of information gained
• guidelines for schools
• new documentation relating to legal duty of care.

The new guidelines for schools contain the following information for planning and managing school visits (*see* pages 81–5).

(**a**) Is the visit necessary? (What is its purpose; does it fit in with school objectives; where can advice be sought; what skills are you looking for in the providers; do they offer value for money?)
(**b**) Does the activity/course offer progression, differentiation, participation and opportunities for recording achievements?
(**c**) Pre-visits or pre-enquiry letters.
(**d**) Risk assessment – is the activity appropriate for the target group?
(**e**) Staff qualifications and experience.
(**f**) Acceptable staff/pupil ratios.
(**g**) Suitable specialist equipment in good order.
(**h**) Seasonal conditions.
(**i**) Pupil vetting – medical questionnaires, special needs.
(**j**) Pupil selection.

(**k**) Staffing – voluntary helpers, First Aid, ratios, pre-meeting, parents' letter/consent, safety plans, trips abroad, insurance.

(**l**) Vetting of centre – accreditation, Health and Safety policy, management and staffing, accommodation and equipment, insurance.

(**m**) Emergency plans for leaders.

(**n**) Legal responsibilities.

(**o**) Further information.

The following could form the basis of a pre-visit/enquiry letter sent to an outside provider.

(**1**) Are the centre's staff familiar with the sites that will be used?

(**2**) What are the procedures for safety; how are they checked?

(**3**) How long has the business been up and running?

(**4**) What is the staff/pupil ratio?

(**5**) Does the centre have qualified medical staff?

(**6**) What insurance cover does the centre offer for its clients?

(**7**) What provision is there for the pupils during bad weather?

(**8**) Is the centre affiliated to any organisations or associations?

(**9**) Who is responsible for safety?

(**10**) What are the qualifications, age range and experience of the staff?

(**11**) What are the procedures for replacing/maintaining the equipment?

When working with children who have been identified as having SEN, one must accept that the work undertaken will undoubtedly be more demanding. By the same token, the rewards can be greater when pupils are seen to be succeeding at a task or developing skills and knowledge.

Pupils may be designated as having SEN for a number of reasons, ranging from sensory and physical difficulties to cognitive and behavioural disorders. Concentrate on abilities the pupils may have and their particular needs to accomplish a task, as opposed to dismissing them from participating due to a handicap. Having said this, it may not be possible to complete all the prescribed activities to fulfil the PoS.

Various strategies are obviously necessary to increase the chances of pupil success and safety in the chosen activity. Pupils with sensory difficulties (for example, visual handicaps) can be assisted by the use of visual aids with brightly coloured information, brail, hand lines, rails or able-bodied helpers for guidance and auditory communications. There are a number of trails set up for the blind – in forested areas, for example – that use smell, sound and touch as the foci for stimulus.

Children with hearing disorders can be assisted if you speak louder and slower, avoid trying to communicate from afar in windy conditions and try to position pupils downwind. Other helpful strategies include removing any background noise, using clear, visual gesticulations, and including sign language where appropriate.

For pupils with physical or motor control difficulties, help may be afforded by using bigger apparatus with a rougher texture to improve grip. Also shorter distances for activities may be advisable. For wheelchair-bound pupils, careful planning is required to ensure that access is possible so that full participation in activities such as orienteering can be maintained. Specially designed ramps and even surfaces contribute to a successful course. For more hazardous pursuits like canoeing and abseiling, specialist equipment is often available.

For those pupils with behavioural disorders, there must be a greater emphasis on safety and the inherent dangers of the activity. Self-evaluation and interaction with other group members should be highlighted frequently for reformation and correction purposes. There has been a tradition of success with this type of pupil in such activities, provided that the activities are well structured and carefully supervised.

Pupils who experience cognitive deficiencies have been seen to succeed with a 'hands on' practical approach. Minimal reference to written text, briefer introductions and large, clear visual aids, help.

In some cases you may have more than one of the disorders outlined above to deal with. Seek to exploit the most prominent skills possessed by the pupil and structure the activity accordingly.

Working with SEN pupils, one would hope for more support from specialist staff and for smaller groups. SCOPE (formerly The Spastics Society) and the British Sports Association for the Disabled will be able to offer further advice and guidance. If the PoS are extended to include hazardous outdoor pursuits such as climbing, canoeing, etc. then it would be advisable to contact the governing bodies for the sports.

FURTHER READING AND USEFUL ADDRESSES

The list of organisations and publications relevant to this work is quite extensive. All necessary information relating to OAA is contained in the HMSO publication: Department for Education 'Safety in Outdoor Education' (1989, ISBN 0 11 270690 8). This DFE publication is available from:

HMSO Publications Centre
PO Box 276, London SW8 5DT
tel   0171 873 9090.

It is also available from HMSO shops on High Holborn, London, and in Birmingham, Manchester, Belfast and Edinburgh, or from your local bookseller.

This publication is essential reading for all involved in such activities.

British Canoe Union, John Dudderidge House, Adbolton Lane, West Bridgford, Nottingham NG2 5AS

British Mountaineering Council, 177–179 Burton Road, West Didsbury, Manchester M20 2BB

British Orienteering Federation, Riversdale, Dale Road North, Darley Dale, Matlock, Derbyshire DE4 2HX

British Red Cross, 9 Grosvenor Crescent, London SW1X 7EJ

Central Council of Physical Recreation, Francis House, Francis Street, London SW1P 1DE

Countryside Commission, John Dower House, Crescent Place, Cheltenham, Gloucestershire GL50 3RA

Department for Education, Sanctuary Buildings, Great Smith Street, London SW1P 3BT

Duke of Edinburgh's Awards Scheme, Gulliver House, Madeira Walk, Windsor, Berkshire SL4 1EU

English Nature, Northminster House, Peterborough PE1 1UA

Forestry Commission, 231 Corstorphine Road, Edinburgh EH12 7AT

Friends of the Earth, 26–28 Underwood Street, London N1 7JQ

Greenpeace, Canonbury Villas, London N1 2PN

National Association of Outdoor Education, 12 St. Andrews Churchyard, Penrith, Cumbria CA11 7YE

The National Trust, 36 Queen Anne's Gate, London SW1H 9AS

Ordnance Survey, Romsey Road, Maybush, Southampton SO16 4GU

Physical Education Association, Francis House, Francis Street, London SW1P 1DE

Royal Life Saving Society, Mountbatten House, Studley, Warwickshire B80 7NN

St. John Ambulance, 1 Grosvenor Crescent, London SW1X 7EF

SCOPE, 12 Park Crescent, London W1N 4EQ

Sports Council, 16 Upper Woburn Place, London WC1H 0QP

INDEX